POLLARD, E

B/ONA

Please renew/return this item by the last date shown.

So that your telephone call is charged at local rate,
please call the numbers as set out below:

	From Area codes 01923 or 0208:	From the rest of Herts:
Renewals:	01923 471373	01438 737373
Enquiries:	01923 471333	01438 737333
Minicom:	01923 471599	01438 737599

L32b

Hertfordshire Libraries, Arts and Information
L32

D1134254

Jackie

Jackie

BY

EVE POLLARD

MACDONALD UNIT 75 : LONDON

First published in Great Britain in 1969 by
Macdonald and Company (Publishers) Ltd.,
St. Giles House, 49–50 Poland Street, London W.1.

SBN 356 02712 0

Made and printed in Great Britain by
Purnell & Sons Ltd.,
Paulton (Somerset) and London

Set in Monotype Garamond

ACKNOWLEDGEMENTS

It is impossible to enumerate all the sources that have been of help in the writing of this book. But below are some of the most important publications that were valuable:

Jacqueline Bouvier Kennedy by Mary van Rensselaer Thayer. Doubleday 1961.

The Making of the President 1960 by Theodore H. White. Atheneum House 1961.

A Thousand Days by Arthur M. Schlesinger Jr. Andre Deutsch 1965.

Kennedy by Theodore C. Sorensen. Hodder & Stoughton 1965.

The Death of a President by William Manchester. Michael Joseph 1967.

The Report of the Warren Commission. Bantam Books 1964.

The Founding Father by Richard J. Whalen. The New American Library 1964

Robert Kennedy by Margaret Laing. Macdonald 1968.

Onassis by Willi Frischauer. The Bodley Head 1968.

Photographs reproduced by courtesy of Black Star Publication Co., Camera Press, the John Hillelson Agency Ltd. and Transworld Features Syndicate Inc.

To Barry

Contents

1   *In the shadow of Black Jack*   9
2   *The young congressman from Massachusetts*   40
3   *Joe and all the boys and girls*   54
4   *Ladies and gentlemen, your President*   67
5   *At the court of King John*   83
6   *Affectionately, Lyndon*   97
7   *The very First Lady*   118
8   *We love Bobby*   131
9   *Daddy O*   139
10   *Afterwords*   158

Chapter 1

IN THE SHADOW OF BLACK JACK

JACK and Jackie were an ideal couple. She would tag eagerly along behind him, round, wide-eyed face full of adoration. Legs walking as fast as they could to keep up with his long stride. Her hair, dark as blackberries, flapping in the Atlantic breeze. Her wide mouth would break into frequent grins at his wild stories, showing straight white teeth, and her forehead would ruffle in indecision as to whether she should believe him or not. He was her god; she was his acolyte. He was John Bouvier III, and she was his eldest daughter, Jacqueline.

Jackie was born in his thirty-seventh year, a year after his society wedding to Janet Norton Lee, the beautiful daughter of a blue-blooded Manhattan family. Janet's father, and indeed her entire family were of the East Coast snob set. They were in banking and property, with a long register of good works behind them. Janet was brought up in the glittering Twenties, when the world of young girls erupted in the Charleston and fast cars after a close cosseted (and corseted) education. She and her two sisters, the elder, Marion, and the younger, Winifred, were educated in the well-bred straitlaced way of the time at Miss Spence's school in New York, which concentrated as much on the social graces as on the three R's; the ladies obviously expected to concentrate on the former rather than the latter in their later lives. But Janet had staying power, and continued studying a while, for a year at Sweet Briar College, and for another year at Barnard. However, she was by no means a blue stocking, and happily surrendered much of her young life to oop-de-doo Twenty's fun. And riding.

Janet had early become an accomplished horsewoman, and

9

was in the forefront in East Coast women's riding competitions. She also became some competition to her generation at the smart *thés dansants* of the time, and behind the wheel of her own zippy car. Janet Lee was becoming very, very pretty, and when she was at last presented to society, most of whom she of course already knew, in the ultra conventional way at a dance at Sherry's, the wall was not flowered by her beauty. She had emerged, and took the centre of the young socialite floor.

John Vernou Bouvier soon became her suitor. East Coast society being very tightly knit, he had in fact met his future bride many years before when she, a young girl in her teens, became friends with his twin sisters, Maude and Michelle. The sisters, delicate strawberry blondes, were summering with the rest of the Bouviers at East Hampton. Their friend Janet, a lively brunette, was spending the summer with them and her parents Mr and Mrs James T Lee. The girls soon became very close friends, playing tennis, riding and swimming. The eldest Bouvier brother, John, was sixteen years older than his sisters and was well-known in fashionable Manhattan society. In true elder brother style, he ignored their babble, their games and their friend.

John Vernou Bouvier III was tall, well-built for the double-breasted jacketed suits of the Twenties and Thirties, and handsome. By the time he met a very junior Janet Lee, he was already a sophisticated man of the world. He had graduated from Yale University in 1919 and thence entered the New York Stock Exchange as a broker. He had already become known, if not as a woman-fancier, as a man sought after by many women, an intelligent dandy and one of the most attractive, eligible bachelors of the decade. There were many elegant fops dressed as he was, in pale beige blazers and Oxford Bags, silk ties, or tweeds for horseshows—many of them as idle as they were empty-headed—but John Bouvier took his women, and his job, seriously. Never seriously enough for marriage, however, and his friends thought of him

as the constant bachelor. Witty, always dressed in the height of
fashion, moving in the best circles, known to society as 'The
Sheik', or 'Black Jack', because of his year-long suntan, he
never seemed to settle, or want to settle down; and so he lived
until his thirty-sixth year. Perhaps he thought of his success
and wanted a wife and children to whom to pass it on;
besides, by this time most of his friends had married, and even
the most dedicated socialite wants a home to go to sometime.
So home he did go, only this time he noticed his sisters had
grown into women, their young friend too.

Jack had always got on particularly well with women, and
Janet, although she was fully sixteen years his junior, soon fell
under the spell of his charm. The summer after her début she
was being courted by one of New York's most attractive and
sought-after bachelors—a man who had fallen in love with her
freshness and youth. She was flattered, as well she might be, by
the attentions of such a man and soon they fell in love. The
marriage appeared to have been made in the golden heaven of
pre-Depression. The young couple must have looked in the
fluted mirrors fashionable at that time, at Lasata, the Bouviers'
East Hampton summer house, and smiled. The sun seemed to
shine on their lives, and it did not disappoint them on their
wedding day, 7 July 1928. Janet was twenty years old.

The wedding took place at East Hampton, in St. Philomena's
Church. Janet wore the conventional but beautiful bridal
gown, round-necked, long-sleeved, the fine lace veil yards
long, severely covering her forehead. Her bridesmaids, six of
them, wore jonquil yellow chiffon dresses, V-necked and mid-
calf length, with short trains trailing the ground behind them
and wide picture hats in green. Marion and Winifred, matron
and maid-of-honour, wore green dresses and jonquil coloured
hats in the same style, and they all carried enormous bouquets
of flowers. A New York social columnist wrote:

Have you ever glimpsed the loveliness of a bed of nodding green
and gold jonquils in the sunshine? Surely you've all seen a stately

bride bedecked in satin, lace and silver? Combine these effects and you'll have a glowing picture of Mrs John Bouvier III, stepping into the sunshine from the door of quaint St. Philomena's Church yesterday with her attendants about her.

There were five hundred smart guests at the midday reception. It was held, mostly outside, in the sunshine, at the Lee House on Lily Pond Lane. Meyer Davis's orchestra played (traditions are kept in the Bouvier family, for the orchestra played again at a Presidential Inauguration night thirty-three years later) and the beautiful couple floated away on the waves of a vintage champagne and a honeymoon cruise.

Both John and Janet wanted a family very soon. Three weeks after their first wedding anniversary this dream materialised when Jacqueline Lee, named after her father Jack and her mother's family, was born. She was born, not in smart Manhattan but in Southampton, Long Island some twenty-two miles west of East Hampton. Her arrival was six weeks late and her mother, tiring of the hot city, had gone to East Hampton for the weekend. The birth of the future thirty-first First Lady of the United States took place in a typically American hospital, local, small and efficient. John Bouvier, always an adoring father, was a frequent visitor to the hospital and later to her nursery at home, where she was ensconced in a beige wicker bassinet frilled with peach-pink *point-d'esprit*. The parents had decided, according to Roman Catholic practice, that the children should be brought up in that religion, although Janet was Episcopalian, and thus Jacqueline Lee Bouvier was christened at the Church of St. Ignatius Loyola in New York. Her cousin, Michel Bouvier, named after the first Bouvier to reach America, was godfather. Jacqueline wore an embroidered christening gown from Paris, first worn by her grandfather James T Lee, which had a long skirt, puffed sleeves in finest lawn and was strewn with embroidered bouquets. Her birth was, of course, recorded in the Manhattan society columns. This was *de rigeur* . . . her background was after all very rich, very Republican, admittedly Catholic but socially impeccable.

The Bouviers' American lineage hails back to 1814. Twenty-four young Bouvier adventurers came over with General Lafayette's revolutionary army from France, to fight alongside the Americans in their War of Independence against the hated British in 1778. Five years later, the war won, they returned to France but not without some spirited tales of the New Frontier. André Eustache Bouvier, Jacqueline's great, great, great grandfather, told them to his son, Michel Bouvier, who later came to Philadelphia. Philadelphia was, at that time, a burgeoning city in Pennsylvania, full of opportunities for bright, hard-working young men to earn success. Michael Bouvier soon joined the ranks of these. He set up what was soon to become a thriving business, importing all kinds of goods from Italy, particularly Italian marble; he then married one Louise Vernon and settled here with his family to live. The Bouviers were here to stay.

They became prominent citizens of their new country, Jackie's grandfather, John Vernou Bouvier Jr. was a famous trial lawyer and an authority on George Washington. It was the brilliant rhetoric of his speech at the dedication of the George Washington Bridge which made his heirs and all the Bouvier family thereafter refer to it as 'our bridge'.

The family moved forward into the upper echelons of East Coast society. And strangely enough for history, the simplest name was used by most of their men; Jackie's great-grandfather, grandfather and father were all baptised John.

Jacqueline grew up in a happy atmosphere. She had her own nurse, who in the summer would look after her at East Hampton, and in the winter take her and her black Scottish terrier, Hootchie, for walks round Central Park, not far from their large apartment on Park Avenue. Jackie's fastidious interest in clothes must have started right then, for she always wore white gloves, well-tailored coats sometimes trimmed with fur, and matching leggings and bonnet.

Thus Jackie lived, the greatest events of her young life being her birthday parties. The second, which was written up in a New York social column, was her entrance into a dog-show competition at East Hampton where reporters noted:

Little two-year-old Jacqueline Bouvier toddled to the show platform and exhibited with great pride a wee Scotch terrier of about her own size!

Loving Papa was also there, and the dog-show report continued with:

Mr Bouvier is so deeply tanned with East Hampton sun that he much resembled one of those handsome Egyptians you see careening along in their Rolls-Royce cars in Cairo, in the land of the Nile.

Jack Bouvier had obviously scored with a lady again!

When Jackie was three-and-a-half, Caroline Lee Bouvier was born. For Jackie she was almost a plaything, as lovable as Jackie's favourite rag doll, Sammy. Jackie was thought by the family to be very bright, and there is nothing uncommon in that, but perhaps Jackie was brighter than most little girls.

Even at the age of four, dramatic adventures like getting lost in Central Park left her unmoved. Bright and very precocious, she was already perfectly sure of her telephone number. When she was picked up by a passing policeman, she was the calmest of a trio consisting of a distraught nurse and worried parents; she kept her sangfroid. She was not lost; it was her nurse who was lost. The nurse, like all nannies to wealthy heirs and heiresses, knew that Jackie would be a worthy catch for any kidnapper. This family tale, though amusing, shows one of Jackie's strong points, a certain independence. It also shows how much the house circled round the little girls, with Jackie making the running.

The sisters were already quite good friends when young; Jackie's name for Lee was 'Pekes', and Lee called Jackie 'Jacks'. Jacqueline, like most first-born children, was the stronger, more independent character. Lee, as she soon came to be called, like most younger siblings, was slightly more babyish, used to being the youngest and to being a little more taken care of. She grew up quieter and more diplomatic. Jackie would tell the whole truth and nothing but the truth. Not for her the lisp and the sugar-coated, childish *bon mots* of other little girls. If someone wore something unusual or looked slightly funny, Jackie would not hesitate to chirp up noisily and remark upon it. She was definitely not a diplomat. And as she became more voluble many ears were turning pink at her straight talk.

Schooldays arrived at last for Jackie, probably to the great relief of the Bouvier nurse. Along with a generous sprinkling of the daughters of the well-to-do she went to Miss Yates's Kindergarten in New York, and then, a year later, to Miss Chapin's School, a private school with three hundred girls and a uniform of navy blue. Here they were taught, besides the rudiments of knowledge, all the rules of 'naice' young ladies.

This ladylike school doled out as its most dire penalty a 'talk' with the then headmistress, Miss Ethel Stringfellow. Jackie, during her time there, was to have many of these talks, which marked her as something of a rebel. She was bright and slightly precocious, used to spending a great deal of time in the company of grown-ups and accustomed to learning from them easily and early. Apart from her parents there were two sets of grandparents, many uncles and aunts and older cousins, and of course the ubiquitous nurse. Their interest and attention made her too quick at school, and when she learnt things and had finished them before the others, she was not of a nature to sit quietly and wait. She was just plain mischievous. Miss Stringfellow and she had many of these heart to hearts, all of which, of course, were kept secret from her mother, who only discovered her daughter's naughty behaviour when she remarked brightly to one of Jackie's friends how naughty Jackie was. She received the unnerving reply that she was, and in fact seemed the very worst girl in the school! The 'friend' joyfully recounted how Jackie was sent to the headmistress the most frequently of all. Janet, knowing her daughter, should not have been very surprised. At Lasata, the East Hampton home of her grandparents, Jackie was always getting into scrapes, but she questioned her daughter nonetheless. Jackie, realising her mother knew, tried to make the best of it by giving this casual description of her 'talks' with the headmistress. Her bravado was real and not fake. Authority at that time really meant very little. She hardly heard the headmistress's words, let alone heeded them. Miss Stringfellow was not getting through. Not yet. The teacher was well aware of Jackie's insouciance but finally she found a way through it—by means of Jackie's favourite hobby, horses. Because of her mother's skill as a horsewoman, Jackie had soon learned to ride and, to her mother's delight, she quickly became both expert and keen. When Miss Stringfellow described her pupil as a thoroughbred the metaphor was a good one. Jackie had the brain and graceful build, as well as the tenacity and speed of a true thoroughbred. But even a thoroughbred, if unbroken and untrained, would never be able to run a race or even pull a cart. Jackie understood this well, and mentally kept the picture fixed in her mind. Her 'talks' with Miss Stringfellow soon became unnecessary. The filly, though high-spirited, was learning sense and was becoming a leader.

Jacqueline herself always said that her headmistress at Miss Chapin's had been 'the first, great moral influence' in her life. In turn Jackie's old adversary admitted that her patience was tried very hard with the headstrong girl, but that her wilfulness also included a will to learn, to enquire, to understand. And this was so, for apart from the usual little-girl books, like those of Beatrix Potter, A A Milne and such, Jacqueline, at the age of six, was quite up to borrowing a book from her parents' bookcase whilst supposedly taking her afternoon nap. One she selected was a book of short stories by Chekov. Her mother, being told by her daughter that she had enjoyed the story,

The Lady with the Dog, was amazed that the child should have persisted with the story, full of long and complicated Russian names, and that she had understood it. This was the beginning of Jackie's lifelong, voracious reading. She was not a sit-at-home, however, and the long, hot summers were spent swimming and riding, as well as reading. From her earliest years Jackie combined varied aesthetic, intellectual and physical tastes. Her father encouraged her in this, as he encouraged his daughters in everything, helping them with schoolwork, allowing them to keep pets; he even let Jackie keep a rabbit in the bathroom of their Park Avenue flat! He was often to be seen at the end of a lead line with Jackie astride on Rusty, a pony, or Jerry, a miniature horse belonging to the local riding stable. Soon she was able to ride without this guidance . . . and soon she became a brave jumper.

At five, already a sporting Bouvier competitor—the competitive feeling in America amongst large families was not confined only to the Kennedys of Boston—Jackie entered the Family Class competition at the East Hampton Horse Show with her mother. Both very attractive on chestnut mares they pulled off the Third Prize. Her mother, used to entering top-flight jumping competitions, and winning, took great pride in this minor event. Jackie was really following in her mother's four-legged footsteps. Dressed in a junior version riding habit, jodhpurs, white shirt and leather gloves and boots, her dark eyes flashing as she took on arduous jumps in competition with girls several years older, Jackie seemed every inch Janet Bouvier's daughter. Janet herself had been headlined at riding shows as 'A Picture of Grace and Skill' and sartorially was a leader on the riding scene—a current report of the time says:

She wears the very smartest in riding habits at Long Island horse shows. She is shown here in complete costume: top hat, Ascot tie, coat with contrasting collar and trousers to match the collar. Long leather boots, of course.

Janet also instilled physical bravery and courage into

Jacqueline. They both took their knocks in the riding ring. Jackie, aged six, entered a jumping competition and, when she fell off her horse, about to go crookedly at a fence, she furiously got up and was desperately trying to scramble back into the saddle on the wrong side when a horse show official reached her. The spectators, admiring the brave little girl, applauded. Jackie seems to have liked well enough the roar of the crowd for, on the way home, she suddenly turned to her mother and coyly asked why the crowd applauded when she fell off. Her mother quickly responded by saying they were very silly people who did not realise that Jacqueline had handled her pony badly, letting it go at the fence from a wrong angle. The pony could have been hurt, she said, to a now chastened Jackie.

Nonetheless, the Bouviers could not resist taking pride in their daughter's equestrian success. If she was not riding she watched as much as she could, often accompanying her father, and at seven she earned the title of Long Island's youngest horse show fan. She could reel off the names of competitions and their winners as fast as her multiplication tables. Even *The New York Times* was finally drawn to her since she won the two main competitions for young people at Madison Square Gardens, The American Society for Prevention of Cruelty to Animals' Good Hands Competition and the Alfred Maclay Trophy for Horsemanship. *The Times* wrote, 'Miss Bouvier achieved a rare distinction. The occasions are few when a young rider wins both contests in the same show.'

Jackie did not, however, concentrate on riding alone. Miss Chapin's school proved to be a fine one and encouraged her imaginative, dreamy nature. At drawing class her sketches were impressionistic, but in writing her stories were set in the present, with a young whimsical touch. She wrote her first poem at the age of eight. As her subject she chose the traditional one of Christmas. There was nothing precocious about her treatment. Santa Claus, reindeer and falling snow all featured in the plain verse which was only eight lines long. But simple exercise though it was, the result showed that Jackie had worked hard at the discipline of rhyming and meter and she was clearly a diligent pupil.

But the little girl had a tomboy streak in her as well. The lawns of Lasata saw her, pigtails flying, climbing trees and exchanging blood-brother oaths with her cousins. She kept up with the boys as much as she could. She worshipped her godfather 'Miche', himself only nine years her senior, who took the place of the elder brother she always wanted. To his precocious cousin he must have looked wonderfully glamorous; he was always taking girls out, going dancing, and was, since the early death of his father, rather wild.

Jackie was fascinated by dancing, and loved dressing up for Miss Hubell's ballroom dancing lessons, which took place at the Colony Club. These fashionable afternoons were graced by little boys, all shining clean faces, Eton jackets or neat blue suits, and girls in pretty party frocks, with hair, like Jackie's, let down in a wavy fall. Crisp white gloves and shrill cries of delight were the order of the day. At Miss O'Neill's ballet classes the lessons were something else. Leotards and ballet shoes were worn, and classical ballet was taught to a background of silence and classical ballet music: Tchaikovsky, Adam, Delibes. Jackie took her ballet very seriously, even to the extent of thinking that one day this might be her career. She took part in recitals and once danced a solo in Debussy's *Gollywog Cakewalk*. She collected a library of ballet stories and was fascinated by costume and backdrop designs. She also steeped herself in romance. She read *Gone with the Wind* three times and took up Lord Byron with a passion. She was a joyful and, in many ways, vehement girl with strong ideas and strong emotions—she adored her father. But at the age of about eight she began to slide further into her escapist hobbies: books were eaten up and she became more withdrawn. Jackie had problems. And so did her parents.

When John Vernou Bouvier III had married Janet Norton Lee, notwithstanding her beauty and impeccably rich and socially acceptable background, smart Manhattan society was still very much surprised. He still kept his many links with it; for a start he and his wife lived in a small but smart New York apartment and he worked on the New York Stock Exchange on Wall Street throughout the year. During the summer, when his family spent the time at Lasata on Long Island, he was a frequent visitor to his clubs. He then was given a flat on fashionable Park Avenue. A duplex, it had enough room to contain Jackie and a nurse, a housekeeper and rooms to entertain lavishly. This was a present from James T Lee, who thought that his granddaughter Jacqueline should have a secure background and home base. The flat was in an apartment block he owned. Number 740 Park Avenue, the flat high in the clouds, was a centre for the *jeunesse dorée* of the time. Cocktail and dinner parties were a regular feature until 1929.

The Twenties were a prosperous decade for the United States. The downtown commercial centres of many big cities were built, radio arrived, new roads were constructed to accommodate that miraculous new gadget the motor car, and the newest fads were gin and jazz. But this was a boom that could not last, the splendid climax of the years before the Wall Street crash.

John Bouvier was a stockbroker and the boom years were great ones for Wall Street. By 1929 more than five million shares changed hands every day and share prices were rocketing. Wall Street, the home of the New York Stock Exchange, became the centre of the frenzy of speculation that gripped America. People all over the country were putting their savings into shares, in the sure expectancy that prices would rise and that a sale would at least double their money. The more people bought shares, the richer stockbrokers like John Bouvier became because they are paid on a commission basis from sales of shares. Once the supply of customers for shares ceased, the price of shares (based on demand) would stop rising. If it stopped rising, then people would sell to make their profit, and if a lot of people sold at once then prices would fall. Well, fall they did and the landslide was deafening. Thousands of people lost fortunes, but worse still, unemployment increased dramatically in all countries doing business with the USA. This was the famous Wall Street Crash which heralded the great Depression—the time of bread queues, hunger marches, mass unemployment, riots and the rise to power of Fascism in Germany.

In July 1929, when Jackie was born, Wall Street was enjoying its last great splurge before the Crash. During that last summer of the gay Twenties, about a million people were gambling on the Stock Exchange, and a lot of them became very rich—for a time.

It started in October, the rude awakening. John Bouvier did not lose everything in the Crash. He did not have to stand in Wall Street and sell his car for a hundred dollars in an attempt to try and pay his debts, as some men did. He was not fished out of the East River with a stack of IOU's in his pocket. Jack had been careful, and had transferred some stock into cash. But he still ended up taking a terrific loss. Humiliated and unable to lower his style of living, he went cap in hand for money—first to his own family, from whom he could only obtain twenty-five thousand dollars, and then to his in-laws, with whom he had never got on terribly well. Despite having taken a flat from his father-in-law, he now obtained cash. But for Black Jack the price was heavy. Obliged to cut down on the club memberships and his scale of living, he was thrown increasingly into free time with his family. His delight in being a father made this enjoyable to him, but the fact that his choice in life was cut down always galled him. In spite of shortage of money, however, Jack retained a stable of horses, mostly for Janet's show jumping competitive events and for Jacqueline's burgeoning interest.

His family, too, were finding life difficult and it was hard to adapt to a new life. The large house Lasata was kept up in exactly the same way as it had been in the pre-Crash days. Five servants were, they felt, really necessary. Nothing was sacrificed to the cause of economy, while their capital, frittered away on the up-keep of the house, got smaller and smaller. Soon they would not be rich, but they closed their eyes and delved into their pockets all the same.

The continued Depression was hitting Jack hard. The fact that he still had about thirty thousand pounds, while many Americans were starving, did not impress him. He blamed his continued losses on the new Securities Exchange Commission, set up to ensure that a crash could never happen again and to control the Stock Exchange Brokers. The man leading the Commission had been a broker and knew all the workings of the Stock Exchange. The loop-holes by which brokers had made quick and painless profits were now efficiently closed. Black Jack vehemently hated this man President Roosevelt had installed. He was, of course, Joseph P Kennedy.

Struggling against their financial loss, he and Janet had their second daughter, Caroline Lee, in 1933. But it was not until 1935 that Jack was getting out of hot water financially. His great uncle had left him a thriving stock brokerage business. He was back in the money again and perhaps this enabled him to go back to his old ways. Black Jack, the gay bachelor, had known fun in New York too well for too long to give it up. And this brings us back to Jackie's problems. Already, aged eight, her youthful happiness was shattered by the first of many blows. Janet and Jack were decided on a trial separation. Neither of them wanted it but it seemed inevitable. In October 1936 they finally agreed to it. Janet would retain custody of Jacqueline and Lee and they would stay on at the 740 Park Avenue flat. Jack moved down to the Westbury Hotel, but he had access to the children at any time he liked 'at all reasonable times and places' and 'on Saturday afternoons and Sunday mornings as he may wish'. He was to pay all bills and debts contracted by his wife before 1 October and one thousand and fifty dollars a month for support of the three Bouvier ladies. Jack was also to pay all dental and medical bills plus everything for the children's education. The dollar, always important in America, was worked out to its last separation cent.

Jack, the man about town, resumed his old ways. Janet cared for her children, never leaving them and worried lest the separation upset them. Jacqueline took it badly. She adored her father. Her parents, however, had been optimistic, and with the simplicity of the young she was sure it would work itself out. After the six months were over Jack and Janet tried again to live together. It took less time than their separation, five months, in fact, to show them it just was not possible. The split was forever. Jack had never been able to become a husband, and Janet could not take the heartbreak. Their lives, in any case, had always been so different and their tastes had always been so opposed. Janet, with her conservative refined taste, her joy in riding, her simplicity, and Jack, swash-buckling, flirtatious, caring little for conventions, enjoying the delights of the big city and the smart life, were hardly made for each other's happiness. The strongest thing between each of them was their love for their children. The strongest hurt these children had to suffer was the split in the family.

Thus Jackie, latterly the noisy one, the tough little girl of the riding ring, became more shy and quieter. She still rode, but often to escape the over-zealous care of a family knowing she was, and feeling she was, deprived of a father. She was a solitary rider around East Hampton, and later, when her father kept a horse for her in New York—an extravagance of the highest degree—around Central Park. She spent more time writing poetry; perhaps her longing to go away is expressed best in a poem she wrote at ten, called *Sea Joy* which, full of childish melancholy, vowed that her only wish was to live by the sea.

Jackie and Lee at this time grew closer and Jackie became a little more like her sister as she quietened down. The events of grown-up lives, slightly strange as they were, edged them closer to one another. Divorce, in any family, is sadly harmful to the children and life now became a constant emotional tug of war between mother and father, which could not have been eased by the adoration of Jackie and Lee for their father. He lavished praise on them as he would on a woman and courted them in the same manner. Once separated from their mother, he was to use these talents to the full to capture their undying love and attention. Divorce was also something to be ashamed of in their set. The socially impeccable backgrounds of school friends and the family stability of cousins made them feel outcasts.

At an age when children wish to conform, Jackie had to set her face against the world through no fault of her own. It was a lesson she was not to forget. Her childhood was slowly ending. She was growing into an intelligent though sensitive girl, still interested in horses and the ballet, but much more introspective than she might perhaps have been without the divorce. Her parents, of course, did their best to cushion her against as much of the after-effects of the separation and, later on, the divorce, with time spent with both Lee and Bouvier relations, and her beloved Danseuse, her mother's hunter on whom she had won many a competition. But Jackie never really did get over the partial loss of her father. Her eyes, even now, glitter when anyone talks of him; he died in 1957. 'He was a most devastating figure,' she says of him, and that he was.

Jack's skill at wooing his daughters came into full play after the separation. He, of course, had had a great success with the ladies in his bachelor days; he had also been one of the cleverest men at Yale. In fact he had taken much after his father, John Vernou Bouvier II. But Black Jack was much more the European than the Anglo-Saxon. Certainly he was not the typical American. His behaviour, with those women he loved, and with money, which he spent casually, was Latin or Gallic.

Of course, it was from France that his antecedents came. The first inkling of this was in his looks—he would concentrate much effort and time on his tan, but even when not tanned his dark features would look more Latin than anything else.

His attitude, too, was European; he took the strict European view of daughters. They had to be interested and interesting. They were always to be turned out as beautifully as possible, no American joking at scraped knees and cute pigtails for him, and even his daughters were to be women of elegance and mystery from their earliest days. They, wanting to attract his compliments, did their very best to live up to his wishes. Their father deliberately encouraged their growing knowledge of horses and dogs, he let them ride bicycles with no hands and gave them gourmet sweets only if it meant being mischievous in front of their nurses. He did not encourage them to conformity. A Sunday with Jack was much more exciting than a week in school and a fairly sedate Saturday with their mother, and well he knew it. When the girls eventually moved into a smaller flat near Miss Chapin's school, Jack, afraid that the memories of them all living under one roof would recede completely, doubled his efforts to stay in the limelight in his daughters' lives.

Jackie and Lee spent half of every half-term holiday and six weeks in the summer with him, apart from every Sunday. He would come to collect them in a superb sports car and a special signal on his car horn—a series of long and short toots, which both the ladies can whistle even today—heralded his arrival. At East Hampton he had organised baseball games, promoting the Bouvier Black Ducks against fisherman Kip Farrington's Mugwumps. He told them stories about Europe and often recounted the romantic adventure of Michel coming to America after his father and uncles had fought in the American War of Independence. He introduced them to sophisticated gourmet delights, such as pistachio ice cream, and encouraged them to learn and see as much as possible.

He was, above all things, as are all men successful with women, a good listener. When his daughters were anti-vivisectionist, he helped them compose telegrams to the press. When keeping a dog in their new smaller apartment was impossible, he arranged with the local pet shops for his daughters to take for walks whatever dog on sale they felt the sorriest for. Sometimes the three of them would go to Baker's Field at Columbia University and they would play in the outdoor rowing seats set up for sculling practice. Or they would watch baseball tryouts. Often a whole crocodile of girls were given lunch at Schraffts, off to a film, then on to a big delicious ice-cream sundae. Jack was forever proudly introducing his daughters, to jockeys at the paddock of Belmont Park, a fashionable race track, or to business colleagues at lunch in Wall Street, near the Stock Exchange.

Jacqueline, who was growing up in looks just like himself, still loved to ride, and Jack, who kept a horse for her in New York, would often ride with Lee and Jackie in Central Park. He indulged their whims and gave them accounts at Saks and Bloomingdales, the smart department stores, plus a small monthly allowance. They were frequent visitors to the Bouvier relations. Thus Jackie and Lee kept in close touch with their many Bouvier cousins. It was not all plain sailing, however, for, encouraged by their father, their manner was more subtle and subdued than is usual in American children—and they were more elusive, a quality that the romantic Jack Bouvier encouraged in his daughters and found attractive in the women that he loved. Lee and Jackie learned this lesson well, with the result that they both have a certain mystery about them to this day. In the America of peanut butter, glee clubs and girly groups he held the sisters slightly back from the rest of the family, yet when an occasion came—their twin aunts' birthday or an anniversary—the beautiful three would be sure to turn up, and make a stunning entrance. 'Isn't it wonderful that Jack and his children are here!' someone would be bound to say.

Inevitably, Jack would praise them in front of everyone else in the family. He would come out with such remarks as, 'Jackie's got every boy at the club after her and the kid's only twelve ... what are we going to do with her when she's twenty?' He would remark on their prettiness or their cleverness and for him they were never in the wrong. As for the other members of his family, his sisters would say nothing, his father would simply smile, he was fond of all his grandchildren, but the rest of those grandchildren rather grew to dread lunches, and perhaps envy the sisters this fulsome public praise which they named Vitamin P, the cure-all praise pill. The two sisters could hardly fail to do well on it.

Thus, despite the divorce, Jack's relationship with his daughters was stronger than most men's with their female offspring. Like many French or Italian men who are seen discussing subjects such as love, war and clothes with their daughters, almost as urgently as if they were their young mistresses, Jack took his daughters to him. Jack looked the epitome of a successful middle-aged man with a beautiful young girl-friend. The girls could take him into their confidence, discuss anything with him; not for them the generation gap or the things never spoken about.

Nevertheless, Jackie did suffer in many ways from her parents' separation and she started to learn the hard facts of life early. Some respite from grown-up squabbles, even though diplomatically conducted by Jack and Janet, came when she was sent away to school in Connecticut.

Janet had remained very much the devoted mother during the entire separation and divorce crisis, but she was powerless to prevent her daughters' unhappiness and could not compete with Jack's extravaganza either financially or emotionally. Being quieter, more retiring, and more of the old school than her husband, she could only, in her quiet way, be just as much an example to her daughters as he was. Life must have been hard for her at this time, particularly with two young children to care for. But Janet was still a beautiful woman, and she was not to remain alone for very long. Eventually, in June 1942, she married Hugh D Auchincloss.

Hugh D Auchincloss was the very opposite of John Vernou Bouvier III. He was tall, ruddy complexioned and wore glasses. He was gentle, conventional and correct—a gentleman in every sense of the word. The descendant of two Glaswegian brothers who made their fortunes in America early in the nineteenth century and settled in Newport, Hugh studied at the Yale and Columbia Law Schools and, in the early Thirties, entered Government service, applying his fine Scottish legal brain to diplomatic documents. During the war he worked on a naval assignment and later he set up a stock brokerage firm in Washington. He soon became very successful in this and owned two beautiful houses. The winter house, Merrywood, was in Virginia near to Washington DC, across the shore from the Potomac, near some of the most beautiful country in America where Maryland, West Virginia and Virginia meet— a land of huge trees and flowing rivers. It was a dignified Georgian house set amid woods.

In the summer the family would go to Newport, fashionable Newport, to Hammersmith Farm, a comfortable farm, although large, with huge Victorian-size rooms. When the family moved there, it was quite a family. Hugh Auchincloss had three children from his previous marriage—a son, a little older than Jackie, called Hugh Junior but always known as Yusha, of whom Jackie became very fond, and Nini and Tommy who were younger. Jackie and Lee fell into happy line with this new family.

Thus the family settled into Merrywood, a large house, full of lovely rooms and with forty-six acres of private grounds. There is a swimming pool, an enclosed badminton court and a small stable which soon became a comfortable home for Danseuse. This was Jackie's first taste of Washington life and she enjoyed her time spent there with the large Auchincloss family. She writes, much later at twenty-three, on the occasion of her mother's and step-father's tenth wedding anniversary of the decade they had shared together. The enmeshing of the five children, the Auchinclosses and the two Bouvier sisters. The existence of their half-brother and sister, who shared the love of them all. The stability, the one thing Jackie had missed was present, she loved the warm corners of the large rooms at Merrywood and the wide expanses at Newport. Jackie so near a marriage of her own saw in her mother and step-father something to admire.

And it was true. The Hammersmith Farm days were fun. The house had been built on Rhode Island in 1888 and once the farm had possessed a thousand acres of land. It originally belonged to William Brenton, the first Royal Surveyor in the United States, who hailed from a then small village just outside London called Hammersmith. Built by an uncle of Hugh's, and acquired by his parents just before his birth, the farm was a legacy to Hugh, but he cared for it like a farmer. There were stables for work horses, a few sheep and goats and Guernsey cows. At one stage corn and hay were grown, but this did eventually become too difficult to keep up. Likewise the elaborate gardens, which Jackie as a young girl would sometimes help to weed. Inside, the house was built for ease. The large rooms held comfortable furniture. Jackie could often be found, almost hidden in an enormous comfortable armchair, reading a book. The walls white, the carpets red, and an already design-conscious Jacqueline decreed that all family dogs should be black to go with the colour scheme! It was a wonderful house for children, with quiet corners to retire to and intriguing stuffed animal heads on the walls and even a stuffed pelican in the Deck room. The house was a family house and much beloved. The children had a sort of Boy Scout/ Girl Guide cameraderie, with so many of varying ages—and eventually a half-brother and half-sister for Jackie were born, Janet Jennings Auchincloss, and James Lee Auchincloss.

Jackie's room had yellow wallpaper with a white border, the furniture, simple and wooden, was white, and her headboard was cane. When young she collected china animals and there was a shelf of these. Her collection of books, which spread as she grew older into classics, poetry, French and Spanish, were also kept here. Often she would sit in this room reading, perhaps her bouvier-des-flandres dog, Caprice (bought by her father because of the name), would be with her. It was from this room that she was to emerge as a bride. But now, at the age of fourteen, her education had to be continued near her new home, and she moved to Holton-Arms School, Washington. It was a day school and Jackie really enjoyed it. She had considerably quietened down since the 'talks' with Miss Stringfellow at Miss Chapin's, and her kindly step-father, who did not encourage any of his children or step-children in mischief, gave her some good advice. Uncle Hugh, as Jackie called him, told her to attend the course given by the best teacher; her interest in the subject was beside the point. With that advice Jackie, not surprisingly, did well in Latin, for she immediately recognised the ability of the Latin teacher, Miss Shearman, and although, along with her fellow pupils, she often thought her too strict and hard, she afterwards agreed Miss Shearman was right. Uncle Hugh's advice also proved right, for she ended up adoring Latin. Jackie also continued with her French lessons which she had been receiving since a small child, and she started a new one, Spanish. She little realised how diplomatically useful they were to be later.

She continued the well worn path of all the well-bred young girls of Washington. Continued dancing lessons, at Miss Shippen's . . . and during the holidays a chance to practise your steps with *real* boys. The genteel dances for the young set fascinated and amused Jackie. She wrote and drew a caricature of herself, remarking on her big feet, a thing thought dreadfully unfashionable and unladylike then. She refers to her first evening dress, in blue taffeta, gold track shoes and her feathered hairstyle, which she found very chic. The latter refers to Jackie's then short, layered hair.

Despite a more active life Jackie continued with her own introspection, painting, drawing and writing.

In a poem that she wrote in her early teens, she gives expression to an adolescent longing to escape and a love of nature. She has composed a poem about the autumn, the feeling of walking along the sea-shore and watching wood-fires burning. These sights and sounds of Long Island evoke nostalgic thoughts, a feeling of solitude and a memory of previous years. Melancholy of this kind is a common enough adolescent feeling but Jackie had been skilful enough in describing it. The last verse reads like a dreamy advertisement for cigarettes in the cinema, and already clothes—to be one of her obsessions—are mentioned to evoke a feeling of the open-air life. Turtle-necked sweaters are linked in the same breath as riding horses and swirling leaves.

These poems were full of wanderlust and the nostalgia of youth—a different sort from that of old age, because it invariably shows a longing for what the child has never known.

Her home life, though, was already crowded out by people, events and the busy social life of a fourteen-year-old. The round included extra lessons and courtesy calls. A mother here and a father there. It is not surprising that her poetry recalls her quieter, more solitary experiences. The idea of a beach where no-one was present appealed to her. Doubtless Jackie had a romantic hero, possibly fictitious, and her poetry composed at this age was certainly romantic.

But she also had an excellent reason for trying to excel at poetry. In this time of flux, torn between her father who struggled hard to keep first place in her affections, and her happy life in the home of her new step-father, a great source of strength and comfort was her grandfather, Grampy Jack, John Vernou Bouvier Junior. The paternal role he was to play in her life was one which would be repeated in later times and by other people.

As in many things, Jackie found someone older to encourage her ideas and even her private, very private hobby of poetry. She found this, where she always had, in Grampy Jack, her paternal grandfather who loved this granddaughter who wrote poetry as he did himself, and wrote him eager, excited letters. Throughout the vicissitudes of her parents, her grandfather was solid as a rock. Grampy Jack was showing Jackie that not only the Auchincloss family had culture and style. True he had always written her exceedingly intelligent and wise letters. But now he had to back this up with something which was a little more intellectual. Jackie was fast being drawn into the quiet corners of Merrywood, books under arm, with these books being Auchincloss books and literary ideas being in the Auchincloss style. Henceforth he was to show her the highest efforts at poetry. The Bouviers were not spectators, but intrepid participants . . . in poetry, riding, swimming and every activity. It was a very American quality and togetherness was part of it. And it was practised in Irish Boston as well.

She would send him her own poetic offerings, and he would give criticism, in a witty epistolary style. When Jackie was twelve years old, he wrote to her that it was a futile labour to gild the lily but it was an equally vain gesture on his part to suggest that her work should be altered in any way. But, he went on to say that he was a powerful technician and that the alterations he had made served to make her verse conform to the rules and regulations of scansion. He complimented her on the cleverness of her ideas and their admirable development. The letter was a humorous one, full of mock-pedantry, and it showed his deep affection for his granddaughter.

When she was thirteen, Grampy Jack (who always wore a high starched collar and pince-nez) encouraged her to keep up a regular correspondence with him.

He viewed her promise that she was going to inundate him with letters with a certain scepticism. Grampy Jack recounted to her a cautionary tale about those noble resolutions which are made after receiving Communion, but are allowed to peter out to nothing when enthusiasm goes. However, he went on to say that he was keen to set up a flow of correspondence between himself and his grand-daughter along the lines of the one between Horace Walpole and Lord Chesterfield. It was an inspiring thought, despite the letter's teasing manner.

Apart from his kind, intelligent interest in his grand-daughter's scribblings, he knew that at this time she would be drawn into another family, the Auchinclosses, and he did not want to lose her from the Bouviers. Jacqueline flourished under his guidance. Later, when she had started Spanish and collected a few swear words like *caramba*, she immediately confided her delight to her grandfather. He responded in his usual witty way. He questioned why Jackie's Spanish teacher should encourage her to swear in that language. He thought the sound of '*Caramba*' was a pleasing one to hear, but he doubted whether its meaning was any stronger than damnation. In fact, the word was so ineffectual as to be meaningless, but if she accompanied its use with dramatic gestures, if she waved her arms about and her bosom throbbed, she might invest '*caramba*' with a significance. But his considered advice was that she should drop '*caramba*' from her vocabulary. It was apparent that Grampy Jack delighted in these letters and the meeting-ground he had with his grand-daughter.

Jackie obviously enjoyed this correspondence and kept it up, as she kept up with her other writings. There was always a poem for someone's birthday, and earlier stories about the family animals were composed in a creative twinkling. These two interests of hers mingled when, at fifteen, she was sent to Miss Porter's School in Connecticut. Her horse, the beloved Danseuse, a family pet since retirement from the world of show jumping, would have to be left behind at Hammersmith

B

Farm, unless she could raise the twenty-five dollars a month for his upkeep at the school. Her family, like wise wealthy ones, kept their children on small allowances, and at the time hers would not cover the cost of 'Donny' at school. Lacking nothing if not courage she wrote to Grampy John Vernou Bouvier Jr. asking if he would treat her to this. As semi-camouflage she enclosed her latest poem for a critique. Her grandfather ignored the poem and went straight to the real point of her letter. He told Jackie that sometimes a luxurious extravagance could be deemed necessary because of the circumstances behind it. He thought it was fair to put Danseuse in this category. The pony came under the heading of a psychological and spiritual prop. And Grampy Jack was willing to pay the 25 dollars per month for her upkeep for this reason. He did not fail to point out that this was an indulgence but agreed that keeping Danseuse justified it. The two were joining forces again.

Of course, times were awful, war was raging in Europe and in Asia, but Grampy knew Jackie's growing predilection for a solitary hour or two away from people. He would rather she were riding than walking on her own and at boarding school she really appreciated the horse. She mentioned her pet in one of her first letters back from Farmington, Connecticut. She wrote that she groomed her every day and went to see her before lecture time. Her flat-mate who was called Sue teased her about her attachment to the extent of locking her in her stall. Jackie pampered Danseuse and went so far as to steal a blanket from another horse in the stable and wrap it around her own charge. Miss Bouvier's money certainly seems to have been stretched tight. At any rate she could not be accused of having led a spoilt childhood.

Jackie enjoyed Miss Porter's at Farmington. The Connecticut countryside was beautiful, and when the girls were allowed to ride through it Jackie's romanticism and love of nature went out to it. The school was also a haven from the complications of family life, far away from fathers, step-fathers and the new Auchincloss household which was gradually and happily settling into one big family. At Miss Porter's she also made some life-long friends.

The background of the school was very old New England. The original Miss Porter had founded the school in 1843, in a small hotel originally designed for canal travellers, bought for a song when trains put the canals out of business. Daughter of a Congregational minister and the sister of Noah Porter, a President of Yale University, she was a very advanced feminine educator at that time. The school flourished and grew, gradually adding other large white clapboard houses of the sort found in New England settlements to accommodate a group of one hundred and ninety privileged pupils. Not only were they privileged from the financial angle, although we have already noted some of them had very small personal allowances, but they all had excellent schooling with the very best teachers, in small classes. A housemother was assigned to each of the seven dormitories, to be part chaperone, confidante, general comforter, a mother figure to her charges. Jackie wrote once to a Farmington friend that she was convinced that no-one would ever marry her and she would end up as a house mother at Farmington. Jackie, like most girls, doubted her marriageability, and as she grew up to twenty, twenty-one and twenty-two when so many contemporaries were already wives, and some were already mothers, she almost saw herself sitting on the shelf! Nonetheless, the only shelves she had to worry about at Farmington were those in the library, the ones crammed with books to be studied for examinations.

Like the rest of the girls, Jackie shared one of the gaily decorated rooms in the dormitory houses, each of which contained twin mahogany beds, desk and easy chairs and, of course, all the personal *bric-à-brac* of the occupants. The girls learnt much beside the basic schooling learnt everywhere else. Accent was put on such housewifely arts as may be useful to a girl who may one day be expected to run at least one fairly extensive household. The girls were taught to wait at table—if for nothing else but to train their servants later on—and were invited to after-dinner coffee with their teachers. Intelligent conversation was encouraged. Every subject was covered, art, politics, history, personalities—all and everything, and Jackie, a great wit, enjoyed these chats very much. Her father, Jack, would come up on Sundays and take his daughter and some of her friends to a steak dinner at the Elm Tree Inn in Farmington, a treat allowed at weekends. Jackie used to say afterwards her friends would line up for these dinners, so popular was he with her school friends.

Generally she was in the seventh heaven for a fifteen year old, she had her horse, her friends, close pals being room-mates, first Sue Norton, then Nancy Tuckerman (still a close friend of Jackie who has acted as her personal secretary for many years now), both of whose parents were friends of her own. And she visited other friends, the Wilmarth Lewises, sister and brother-in-law to Uncle Hugh. Wilmarth Lewis, being an expert on the English eighteenth century, had a huge collection of books. They also did a very good chocolate cake. Between schoolgirl bites Jackie's already great interest in literature was fanned by these two intellectuals, who kept up the good work with a gift of a rare book, often one on art, each Christmas. Even now rare art books are still a favourite gift for Jackie.

Her reports, as usual, were good. Her grades were around the A minus class. She preferred History of Art, taught by Miss Sarah McLennan, to any other class and Jackie was an eager pupil. Likewise Miss Watson's English classes. Her interest in her own writing did not abate, only now her artistic training jumped into her letters in the guise of comic sketches often depicting the headmaster, Mr Johnson; he, to her mother's idea, never praised her highly enough, but to Jackie, he was 'greatly understanding'. Jackie prospered under the expert tuition of her teachers; her great

interest in art was built up into steady foundations of knowledge during these three years. What she accomplished in
mathematics or science is hidden from the world and perhaps,
like so many young girls, the precise interested her less than the
realms of pure creativity and romantic imagination.

If she was wont to fly into both the latter, the letters from her
grandfather, with their salutary reminders of the world to come
and life outside the chintzy windows of Farmington must, have
kept her feet down on terra firma. During her first term he
wrote her a letter which in many respects is a tongue-in-cheek
sermon in the manner of Polonius' homily to Laertes in *Hamlet*.
It is full of tiresomely sensible advice cloaked in fine language
in the genre 'Neither a borrower nor a lender be'. But Grampy
Jack's advice, no matter how entertainingly it was couched and
despite its humour, was meant to be taken seriously. It is
possible that he saw that his grand-daughter was running the
risk of becoming too romantic and remote. He might have
thought she was attempting to escape some of the realities
which in her position she must face before long. In his letter,
Grampy Jack praises the child's adaptability to her surroundings, because it shows a practical philosophy which he is most
anxious that the young Jacqueline should cultivate. He wants
her to realise that the most essential benefit of her education at
Farmington would be her readiness to take on the burdens of
future responsibility. But he is also concerned lest Jackie
should let her developing sense of responsibility make her a
prig, that she should pride herself on being indispensable.

Grampy Jack need not have worried; his grand-daughter at
Farmington was modest. She was, in her own way, a leader;
pretty and clever, she was not at all scared of authority. She
thus accepted a dare to drop a chocolate pie upside down in a
teacher's lap. She, like the others, collapsed into giggles, but the
laughs gave away the stunt to be devilry and not accident. She
was banished from the room. She also became a good 'snitcher'
... a blanket for Danseuse, some fresh baked biscuits for herself

and Tucky, her room-mate Nancy Tuckerman, and she managed to be a clever and charming 'wheedler'. She extricated the original Miss Porter's sleigh which had been in storage for fifty years and trained Danseuse to pull it . . . he was to become useful in the summer to run around collecting ice creams and the like. Not a terrific teamster, she spent little time on sports and athletics, preferring her horse, but she did help run the school newspaper, *The Salamagundy!* and contributed regularly. She also took great interest in the school drama group, *The Players*. A friend remembers that she could learn anything in a minute. At study hall she would finish first of anyone—then she would spend the rest of her time sketching—and writing poems.

Jackie emerged from pigtails to beautiful long hair, despite various expeditions into the short feather cut fashionable at the time. She was tall, thin and very pretty, with a clear, pale olive skin. Her large eyes, shining from the outdoor life, made her an attraction in any room. Towards the end of her time at Farmington she did have some male visitors whose presence was allowed only between two o'clock on Saturday afternoon until after tea at the headmaster's house. The tea with the headmaster allowed for subtle vetting. Mostly, the young men were friends of the girls' families whom they had met at holiday dances and such like, and they often travelled from Yale or Harvard to the girls' boarding school in Connecticut. Bright young men, lucky enough to have just missed the war, they would roll up a little bashfully in their first cars. Jackie received her visitors gleefully. They were often the friends of Yusha Auchincloss, but if any of them pierced her heart she never recounted it to paper, poem, or friend.

The fact that she was often a little quieter than her school friends, and that perhaps she had a stronger relationship with her father and grandfather, both men much older than she, was put down to her parents' divorce. The void created by the partial loss of her father could never be entirely filled although she was surrounded by love and had a devoted stepfather. Her time of absolute security in the family she was born into was very brief but at school in Farmington she was happy. At the end of her time at the Connecticut school in the schoolbook is the legend:

JACQUELINE LEE BOUVIER
Merrywood
McLean, Virginia
'JACKIE'

Favourite song:	*Lime House Blues*
Always saying:	'Play a rumba next'
Most known for:	Wit
Aversion:	People who ask if her horse is still alive. Donny had died whilst she was at the school
Where found:	Laughing with Tucky
Ambition:	Not to be a housewife

Little did she know. As she stepped out of the school gates for the last time, without Danseuse, to go home and prepare for her début she did not realise how easily she was to achieve her ambition.

Chapter 2

THE YOUNG CONGRESSMAN FROM MASSACHUSETTS

DÉBUTS in America exist just as they do in England and Europe generally. It is the upper crust entrance to the marriage market and the girls are groomed for it as yearlings for a rodeo. The yearling herself, apart from the right background, needs no special qualities; if she is pretty so much the better, the job will, it is presumed, be easier. If she is clever, it matters not at all. Thus it was with Jacqueline Lee Bouvier.

She left school and spent five months at the summer house, Hammersmith Farm. These were the last days of childhood—and the long summer days were spent dancing around, riding and playing with her three year old half-sister and her baby half-brother, Jamie, who was born during Jackie's last term at Farmington. She visited the Bouviers at East Hampton, and made trips to New York for shopping sprees and visits to her father. The season as such for a young girl was filled with other débuts, dances and tea parties with friends of her parents. In those days young people did not lead lives of their own, going out together, spending their own money, but lived very much in the shadow of their parents, waiting impatiently to be counted as adults too. Time spent with older men and women would have been boring to most girls but Jackie seemed to enjoy it well enough.

Her début was a tea party, which she shared with her step-brother who was christened on the same day. After the christening at Trinity Church, with the Dean of the Virginia Theological Seminary officiating (the Bouvier girls were Catholics but their mother and stepfather were not), the family, and many of their friends, repaired to the large house for tea and dancing.

The local paper, the *Providence Journal*, describes the scene:

Miss Jacqueline Bouvier, debutante daughter of Mrs Hugh Auchincloss, made her official bow to the social world yesterday when she was presented at an afternoon reception at the Auchincloss estate.

Miss Bouvier, who had been deluged with floral gifts during the day, received with Mr Auchincloss and her mother. During the reception Mr and Mrs Auchincloss were being congratulated on the christening of their son, James L Auchincloss.

Jackie, of course, knew almost everyone there but she enjoyed herself as usual, and her mother had organised everything with her usual flair and good taste. Both she and her mother dislike expensive dances for what should be a basically family event. Perhaps in 1975 Mr and Mrs Aristotle Onassis will present Caroline Kennedy to the world at such a *thé-dansant*. The afternoon was obviously a great success and the fact that, after this event, Jackie's life would hardly change, was unimportant. In the eyes of the world she would now be regarded as officially grown-up. Later that summer she was to share a dance at the smart, exclusive Clambake Club—one of the rare but typical snob clubs scattered up and down the coast, and the sort of place in which nothing has ever, or if possible will ever, be changed. It is basically a masculine retreat but ladies are occasionally allowed to cross the threshold. They are invited to share the spoils of the fishing success of the members, although the manager and chef Ruby can always be relied upon to produce, if not enough is caught, feasts of bean soup, clam chowder, grilled lobster and deep-dish apple pie.

It was, indubitably, the most elegant place for a coming out dance on the whole of Rhode Island. The building stands on a cliff, overlooking the ocean, and on a summer evening, lit up with fairy lights, the club does bend a little and look romantic. Romantic enough, certainly, for Jacqueline Lee Bouvier and Rose Grosvenor, the debutante daughter of the Theodore Grosvenors, with whom Jackie was, according to fashionable custom, to share her dance. And when it came to choosing Jackie's dress, cost was no object. At eighteen, mindful of her hitherto small allowance—and before her knowledge of couturiers led her to their perfumed salons—Jackie went into town and picked up a white dress off-the-peg. It cost fifty-nine dollars—no bargain indeed, but Janet Lee Auchincloss had wanted her daughter to have something absolutely out of this world. She was a little disappointed that she had not been well enough after Jamie's birth to choose the very important dress with her daughter. The dress, simple though it was, looked beautiful on the great night of the dance. This was the beginning of Jackie's well-dressed era, and her taste for simplicity, the secret of true elegance, was to stand her in good stead. Her dress was in white tulle. The off-the-shoulder neckline was delicately ruched, it was banded at waist and hips with three tiers of delicate embroidery. The skirt, slightly bouffant, swept the ground. She wore white gloves reaching to her elbow and carried a nosegay of bouvardia and sweetheart roses tied with a trailing white satin bow. Her hair, long, curly and chestnut-lit, and her golden skin, easily put her in the forefront of those 'presented' that year; in fact she was chosen by Cholly Knickerbocker, a columnist on the Hearst paper chain, as *the* debutante of the year. The writer, whose real name was Igor Cassini, and who had no idea that his brother, Oleg, was later to design clothes for the First Lady, wrote:

America is a country of traditions. Every four years we elect a President, every two years our congressmen. And every year a new Queen of Debutantes is crowned . . . Queen Deb of the Year is Jacqueline Bouvier, a regal brunette who has classic features and the daintiness of Dresden porcelain. She has poise, is soft-spoken and intelligent, everything the leading debutante should be. Her background is strictly 'Old Guard' . . . Jacqueline is now studying at Vassar. You don't have to read a batch of press clippings to be aware of her qualities.

This was attached to a photograph of Jackie, not in her demure white coming out frock, but in the dress that Lee had worn for that occasion. Lee, being the little sister, had felt a bit left out of all the fun. She decided to wear something she wanted, instead of the frock selected as suitable for a fourteen year old. She came down into the ballroom, a flirty curvaceous vamp in a siren outfit she had cajoled the local seamstress to make. It was pale pink . . . strapless . . . and liberally studded with rhinestones. This was not all. Lee had added very grownup elbow length satin gloves, fingerless, but tied in place by a pointed strap on the middle finger. She was a wow!

Jackie later borrowed her sister's outfit, captured the eye of the journalist and became a junior personality overnight. A New York paper wrote:

Jacqueline Bouvier, Queen Deb of the Year, is being beseiged with offers of all sorts and demands for interviews and pictures—but her conservative family is shying away from all publicity.

Another columnist wrote with an almost audible wolf-whistle:

Jacqueline Bouvier's poise! What a gal! She's the beautiful daughter of Mrs Hugh Auchincloss. Blessed with the looks of a fairy-tale princess, Jacqueline doesn't know the meaning of the word snob!

And it was true. Life had been so sheltered for Jacqueline that she had not yet come into contact with the world the other side of the golden fence, but the lessons she had learnt from her mother and father had paid off. Her mother had taught her the conservative good taste for which she is still admired. Unlike so many other mothers who would have pushed their daughters forward into the spotlight that temporarily shone on them, she did her best to restrain the sudden outburst of publicity. Jacqueline was going to college. She should be exactly the same as all the others.

As for Jack, he was delighted with his daughter's immediate success, and he liked the modest way in which she dealt with it. This was a woman of class and style. He continued to be close to her, to bewitch her with his personality, to talk to her about the men she met, advise her on the clothes she bought. And Grampy was pleased that the letters of long ago had been read and digested, and that Jackie was going to Vassar, instead of merely courting the publicity attendent on success.

Vassar is *the* college for the East Coast rich. It was socially impeccable and intellectually stimulating. She had not the slightest difficulty in obtaining entrance. Her pass marks, when she graduated from Miss Porter's, were in the eighties and nineties, and her college aptitude tests were in the ninety per cent rating. This, the top bracket group, made her eligible for any college and placed her in the elite of the university entrants that year.

The summer had produced its crop of newer, more sophisticated fun, its beaux, boys just a few years older than herself from the Ivy League universities such as Yale and Harvard, but Vassar kept Jackie studiously busy. At weekends, when she could leave, she would be torn between home at Merrywood, her father in New York, and Harvard and Yale dances and parties. She combined the active social life of a debutante and student. Despite most parents' desire to see their daughters settled and married, Jack, possibly already a little jealous of the man who would capture his daughter's hand, and wary of the pitfalls attendent on youthful marriage, counselled Jackie against any hasty marital decisions. He advised her against an early marriage. It was not only his possessiveness that came into it. As a man of the world, he could see his daughter's romanticism. He was scared she would fall in love with a knight in shining white armour, that would not shine up so well in the cold light of a middle-aged day. And he knew that beneath his dreaming daughter was tougher stuff.

In fact, his daughter was not contemplating marriage at all at that stage. Her half-sister and half-brother were adorable and were enough to satisfy any maternal instinct she might have had. And she was not one of those bright Forties girls—

slightly tough-eyed with a sharp-clever word, like the heroines of the films after the war—but gentle and rather dreamy. Jackie, at Vassar, unlike most of her contemporaries, had not yet 'set'. She was, very, very slowly edging herself into the mould. Rather reticent, she was not the life and soul of the party, but was always popular, a girl who could have been a leader, but who preferred to go her own way. To many of her classmates, she was there, she was pleasant, but she did not become a great confidence sharer or a bosom pal to all and sundry. She was constantly finding new interests and extending her already developed interest in the *beaux arts*. She had always been fond of music, the intonations of the Catholic Church music, sombre and splendid, which she had known since childhood; ballet music, and the classical music appreciated by her stepfather and his family gradually found their way into her life. She experimented and found other composers, likewise artists and writers. Yet, there seemed to be so little time to be alone. Jackie's favourite course, and best grades, at Vassar emerged as History of Religion.

She had led something of a mixed religious life. Her father's insistence on a Catholic upbringing for his children, although Janet never became Catholic herself, meant that after the divorce the Bouvier girls often went to church without a parent or older person. Their mother, of course, had helped in their religious observance, and attendance at Mass was encouraged. The study of History of Religion fascinated Jackie at Vassar, and she turned to the religion—possibly for answers in her own life—and certainly bringing a new kind of interest to the religion she had taken rather for granted since childhood.

Looking back, Jackie has always felt that had she gone away less and had fewer callers to absorb her time she might have taken more advantage of the opportunities Vassar gave. Nonetheless, her marks were very good, and in Miss Helen Sandison's Shakespeare lessons, 'the greatest course I have ever had', Jacqueline Lee Bouvier started a love affair with William Shakespeare that is not over yet. Perhaps it was his tales of England, Italy and Denmark, or her fascination with her French ancestry that turned her towards Europe. Grampy had slightly romanticised it by claiming their heritage to be noble. It was not, but it was French for all that. She wanted to see the country from whence the first American Bouvier came. To this end she organised a trip. The chaperone was to be Miss Shearman, with whom she had kept in contact since her Holton-Arms schooldays. The three co-travellers were the twin step-daughters of Edwin F Foley Jr., the then Under Secretary of the Treasury, Helen and Judy Bowdoin and Julia Bissell. The girls outfitted themselves for the Grand Tour like the rich American girls they were—silk stockings, hats, dresses, countless pairs of white gloves. They were going to stun the Europeans with their chic. They did stun them for, in 1948, Europe's clothes were still rationed and in short supply. Carefree and having fun, the girls enjoyed their trip travelling first on the upper deck of the Queen Mary and in first class compartments everywhere else. Foley had been begged to get his step-daughters and their voyaging friends into a garden party at Buckingham Palace. Then as now, Americans stood very much in awe of the British Royal Family. This he did, and yet another pair of gloves, the requisite elbow length, were laid in their vast trunks. The girls were impressed with the Palace, despite the crowds and the rain. Jackie was particularly struck by the regal Queen Elizabeth, now the Queen Mother, whose warm smile made them feel very special guests indeed. The girls had even stood next to Mr Churchill.

After a quick glimpse of England, they went off to France. Here they visited the chateau-country and Jackie sampled the local wines. Then a short excursion to Juan les Pins, a relatively new resort, near Cannes. The Riviera with its ornate hotels, the palm trees, the private beaches and boats of the famous moored near the casino, was then the magnet for the rich and well-to-do from America and the rest of Europe. Then on to Switzerland. The summer scene, snow-capped mountains in the distance and warm blue lakes to hand, Lucerne, Interlaken and then down through the mountain passes and the plains of Lombardy to the north of Italy. Milan, Venice, Florence, Rome. At break-neck speed, in six weeks, they *did* Europe, the last weeks being a great rush around the galleries of Milan, the Uffizi in Florence, the Vatican, the Sistine Chapel in Rome, the glories of Venice. The sunny days passed quickly and afterwards, home in America once more, she was left with a greater longing than before to see Europe—and particularly France—properly and at leisure. She spoke French well, and France had captivated her. Wishing to know it better, she was determined to go there again—and she was lucky enough to find a way both to do this and to continue her studies. A notice on the Vassar noticeboard, about Smith College groups who spent their junior year abroad, gave her an idea. Although Vassar did not participate in such groups, Jackie, undeterred, wrote to the Dean. And her request, because of her high marks, was granted. However, the designated country for the continuation of her studies was not France, but England. Jackie, remaining determined to go to France, decided to overcome the language difficulties, which were the main objection to her continuing her studies in a foreign country. She took extra lessons in French, in order to improve her fluency, and passed the requisite examination with flying colours. She was free to go. She spent the summer at the University of Grenoble before entering the Sorbonne in Paris.

Jackie's eyes were now opened to a new Europe—one that she had not seen before—a Europe of humdrum little bistros and cafés, cheap cinemas and bus queues. Jacqueline's French name stood her in good stead . . . at the Gare St Lazare she was greeted vociferously by an absolutely strange porter. Her name was the same as his daughter's. Writing to her mother, Jackie described how he kept calling her 'Mademoiselle Jacqueline' and talking all the way to the bus. Just as the bus was leaving the porter jumped on and ran down the aisle looking for her. When he found her he shook hands and gave her his number which she could use, should she ever return. Jackie thought this a wonderful welcome.

Grenoble, where she spent her first summer, is a small university town at the foot of the French Alps. Like the other students, Jackie found lodgings with a family, rather than staying in lonely splendour in the five star hotel. The family took her to its heart, and Jackie's summer was a very happy one.

America was then the dreamland of European youth. The passage of the liberating, happy-go-lucky GIs was still remembered with affection. Visiting American students were welcomed by their contemporaries in France, who could still remember the ravages of occupation during the war. To students in France these girls, these gay American girls, were golden coming from a golden land. They would help with translations and compositions taking great trouble to find *le mot juste*, and all, wrote Jackie, for some 'dumb foreigner' who could not do her homework.

Jackie visited a great many other places in France before she enrolled at the Sorbonne. She went to Nîmes, a sunny town in Provence with its famous Roman arena used for bull fights to which Picasso and Jean Cocteau were frequent visitors. And Arles, another Provençal town where Vincent Van Gogh spent his most tragic and creative years. Jackie, always the prodigious writer, wrote of the contrast between the mountains of Grenoble and Arles. She was stunned by the sunshine. The simple people of Provence, their large straw panniers full of the fresh fruit, harvesting peace and tranquillity from the soil. She was struck by their dark looks, their sunburnished skin and their unceasing work. She was struck, she from the richest corner of the richest country in the world, at their ability to laugh.

America, with its sprawling towns and its exploding population, seemed to have less of that facility. She was drawn to seeing the Carmargue as a sort of chic Texas, with ranches and wild red flowers in the sand, the sea and the horses going to the waves, and the wild bulls as tough as the horny-handed French cowboys. Jackie was much affected by the warmth of it all, the colours, the deep blue sky and sea. She was the real American tourist. She was the observer but she loved and understood what she saw. And as her time in France continued she could understand their conversations. The magical trip to the new 'other side of life' was all too short.

Jackie's short glimpse of Provence and its inhabitants, and her reports of what she saw, are reminiscent of the naivete of one of Henry James's adventurous heroines in Europe. She gave a report from Sassenage, a village near Grenoble. Again another letter when she visited a local village. It is well known in the area for its grottos and subterranean passages. Jackie, the well dressed ex-deb, would not hesitate to don waders, or go barefoot through water to see something interesting. She also did not mind an alfresco dance. The girl who wore long white tulle dresses at smart clubs on the East Coast enjoyed twirling in cotton and sandals. And when missing the last bus involved walking five miles back . . . it was an adventure.

The summer was over. The term in Paris was about to begin. Jackie and the other girls from the American university packed their large bags, said goodbye to the families that had so warmly welcomed them into their homes.

The Sorbonne is not the best of the advanced educational establishments in Paris. The brightest students go to the Grands Ecoles or the Polytechnique. The University of Paris, of which the Sorbonne is part, is split up into many faculties. Anybody can enrol if they have passed their *baccalauréat*, the equivalent of the English 'A' level. The Sorbonne is an old building in the Latin Quarter housing the faculties of Science and Literature. In the courtyard stand the statues of Louis Pasteur, the famous French biologist, and Victor Hugo, the great poet and novelist.

The foreign students, especially the Americans, were surprised at the freedom enjoyed by the students, but also at the lack of facilities, organisation and private tuition. The huge amphitheatres where the lectures took place were crowded to the beams. There is, of course, no campus, and students, buried in lecture notes distributed by the remote professors, would huddle in the countless cafés of the Left Bank. Jackie was in the centre of post-war Paris. At the cafés on the Boulevard St Germain, at the *Flore* or the *Deux Magots*, Jean-Paul Sartre and his disciples expounded the existentialist doctrines of limitless freedom and limitless responsibility.

Jackie had preferred to live with a family rather than stay in Reid Hall, a dormitory for American students. Once again, as at Grenoble, she found her way to an aristocratic home, again one which had fallen on hard times. The Comtesse de Renty's life had been ravaged by the war. An ex-concentration camp inmate, she had lost her husband to the Gestapo. After the war her income was very small, as a result of which she immediately opened her house to students. In the winter of 1949–50 Jacqueline Bouvier was one of these. The Comtesse's English was extremely limited and Jackie was obliged to use her fast improving French. Time in Paris passed quickly. And for the first time Jackie really saw how the other half lives. French plumbing, notoriously bad, was not up to the running hot and cold water of East Hampton or Virginia, while the draughts were very constant and cold. The Comtesse and Jackie became great friends and travelled together through Germany and Austria at the end of the Sorbonne year in the summer of 1950.

When she eventually left Paris to travel round Europe, Jackie determined to see as much as she could. She travelled to Ireland and kissed the Blarney Stone, and went to Scotland, crossing Auchincloss country with her step-brother, Hugh

Auchincloss Jr., to the northernmost tip of the British Isles, John o' Groats, a far cry from Manhattan skyscrapers.

Jackie was to return to them soon enough, and not long after her return, she became engaged. The object of her affections was a young man called John Husted Jr., a Manhattan stockbroker. The engagement was brief and later they both agreed it was never really serious. Jackie decided to finish her studies at Vassar and then to find a job. By now she was a sophisticated young woman, passionately interested in writing. Her idle debutante days were over. Having tasted the joys of the gay young life of the social set and found them unsatisfying, she wanted a deeper sense of reality. To that end, like many other young girls with an ear for a sentence and an inquiring eye, she decided to make a career in journalism.

Arthur Krock, a *New York Times* columnist and family friend, was prevailed upon to ask his colleague, Frank Waldrop, then editor of Washington's *Times-Herald*, if he still employed girls as journalists on his paper. Waldrop's opinion of the professional abilities of women in the field of journalism was derisorily low, but the idea had a certain appeal, nonetheless, and he was willing to meet Krock's protégé. In the December of 1950 Jackie went for her interview. Waldrop asked her bluntly if she was just playing at a career or if she was serious. He did not want to train her only to lose her to marriage. Jackie replied that she did not want simply to hang around until she got married. She was determined to make a career. Waldrop, however, was looking for a photographer rather than a reporter pure and simple. Well, what girl with a bit of initiative will admit that she has only ever taken holiday snaps with a Brownie or a Leica?

You may be sure that Jackie was quick into photography lessons. She wanted to be part of the paper and picture snapping was part of the job. The only start she was given was a quick conducted tour of the police stations and the hospitals. Thus set up in knowledge of the worst of city life, she was on her own.

The Washington *Times-Herald* had a column of the kind known in the trade as a 'human interest' column. Called *Inquiring Camera*, it would contain interviews, sometimes with famous people, sometimes simply with the man in the street, on a variety of topical subjects. The questions were light-hearted and often rather inconsequential—tailor-made, in the opinion of the editor, for a woman; for who else would give serious treatment to such material? So far it had been tackled by a man. But Waldrop reckoned that a pretty girl behind a camera could do no harm. Jackie's salary was forty-two dollars and fifty cents per week. Like all first pay-packets it seemed like the first real money she had ever owned.

With the job, the money and the new professional world in which she moved, Jackie's life was changing. She was evolving into a business-like, quietly-concentrating young woman. She still loved to dance and go to parties, but as her friends got married and settled down she gradually spent quieter evenings just talking to people. Her greatest interest still lay in the field of art and she would read almost anything she could lay her hands on. The task of amassing material for her column demanded a certain toughness on her part, a quality from which Jackie, when she was not working, liked to retire, preferring to express herself in her rather soft, fast-talking voice, expensively simple clothes and on a more private level, in her letters and paintings. Meanwhile, her salary having spiralled to fifty-six dollars and seventy-five cents per week, she was making good progress professionally. She was continuing with her studies at George Washington University, and she was continuing to go from Washington to New York for visits to Black Jack and the Bouviers. New York, with its bright lights, theatres, cinemas and shops, was gayer than Washington.

There were many beaux, but nothing much to write home about. One of these had been the very pleasant Charles Bartlett, the Washington Correspondent of the *Chattanooga*

Times. It was a light-hearted friendship, and they had never been in the least bit serious about one another. Charles eventually married a beautiful redhead called Martha. Some time after their wedding, they decided to give a dinner party for Jackie in their pretty Georgetown house. Jackie prepared for the dinner party in the same way as for every other. Simply dressed, her hair dark and shiny, cut to just below her ears in the full 'Italian' hairdo fashionable at the time. She liked the Bartletts and enjoyed small parties where she felt more at ease than at a large crush. At dinner a young man, tall, with a shock of reddish-brown hair, leaned over the asparagus (which she coyly refused to admit was being served that evening). She saw before her, for the first time, the young Congressman for Massachusetts, John Fitzgerald Kennedy. Tall, tanned and handsome he asked her for a date that very evening.

Chapter 3

JOE AND ALL THE BOYS AND GIRLS

THE proposed date did not happen. A friend, unknown to
Jackie, was waiting outside the Bartletts' house. He had seen
her car and decided to wait for her. Jack, never a dueller, fell
back. Jackie, of course, remembered the attractive young
Congressman. Later she admitted, 'it was more than just
meeting someone, it started the wheels turning'. But the
wheels turned slowly and meanwhile there were other men to
whisk her to parties and dances and drives in their new fast
cars. Every day the papers were full of the Senatorial elections,
and Jackie kept a close eye on those of Massachusetts. Jack had
not forgotten her, however, and eventually he telephoned her
and asked for a date. She always said later that his calls would
be mixed in with the sound of coins rattling in a telephone
booth of a New England oyster bar. Jack spent that year in a
mêlée of tea parties, electioneering and parading, which left him
little time for the vagaries of romance.

No two such wealthy families could have been more unalike
than the Kennedys and the Bouviers. The relaxed aristocrats
from East Hampton had had money and social position for
generations, there was no demon of ambition thrusting them
forward; they could relax and enjoy a life of effortless superior-
ity. Not so the Kennedys. John Fitzgerald Kennedy was part
of the latest generation of the Boston Irish. His forebears had
emigrated to escape the poverty and famine of Ireland. Their
children had struggled for financial success and their children,
financial success achieved, fought hard for social recognition.
Power and the Presidency would be the biggest prize of all.

Joseph P Kennedy, father of the young Congressman and

leader of the Kennedy clan, was consumed by ambition. Ambition for wealth—he had seen that without money no progress was to be made in any field—and ambition to conquer the heights of power, both political and social. Boston was the seat of the Protestant East Coast aristocracy. Rose Kennedy, his wife, once wondered aloud when Boston's fastidious ranks would welcome them. There were an awful lot of Kennedys—nine of them to be exact—Joseph P Kennedy Jr., Rosemary, Kathleen, Eunice, Patricia, Robert, Jean, and Edward, besides John himself. And then there were Joe's business tactics, which earned him the nickname the Wolf of Wall Street. Jack Kennedy said, many years later, that he was surprised when anyone who had done business with his father spoke well of him.

Joe's father had started life as a saloon keeper, and Joe, when at Harvard, had not been allowed to forget the social gap dividing the Irish, and other recently arrived minorities, from the established Yankee families. Joseph went into business and amassed a fortune over the years. A backroom capitalist who made money do the work, he descended on Wall Street and muscled in on the groups manipulating the share market. He would help organise stock pools whereby a group of men would buy options on a share at, say, ten dollars, and so publicise it and so deal in it that the innocent public, thinking they were on to a winner, would also buy—and the price would shoot up. The group would then sell, making a huge profit, and the share price would plummet, causing gullible investors taken for the ride to make enormous losses.

Joseph himself had a good instinct for money, however, and he sold his stock holdings before the crash of 1929. A booming growth industry on the other side of the country soon attracted his attention—the movie business in California. He went to Hollywood to produce movies and one of his especial protégées at that time was Gloria Swanson. But Joseph was a financier, and the creative side of the business was not where his real flair and interest lay. He began to build far-reaching chains of cinemas and played an important part in the setting up of the giant RKO, Radio Pictures Corporation. In 1925, he visited London with the aim of buying a production company. The important bankers who controlled it would not even see him. Joseph was not to be put off so easily. He went to Paris where, he had learnt, the Prince of Wales was visiting. He discovered the Prince's favourite restaurant, bribed the waiter to place him at the next table and, when the Prince entered, he rose and strode over to him. He reminded the Prince that they had met at the party of a Mr Tuckerman, during the Prince's recent visit to the USA. The Prince politely enquired if there was anything he could do for him.

There was indeed. Joseph Kennedy got a letter of introduction, the doors of the London bankers were opened, and the deal went through. One point, however. Mr Kennedy had never been to the said party, which was the very last kind of affair he could have got an invitation to and had never met the Prince before. But such minor details could not be allowed to stand in his way.

Joe Kennedy was to return to London thirteen years later, but this time no letters of introduction were needed. He came as American Ambassador to the Court of St James's. He had shrewdly recognised the ability of one Franklin D Roosevelt and been one of his earliest backers. The President, in return for his services, made him Chairman of the Securities Exchange Commission, set up to avoid the abuses that led to the Crash. Kennedy was as efficient at eradicating questionable practices as once he had been adept at exploiting them. In 1938 Roosevelt made him his Ambassador in London.

JPK had left Hollywood five million dollars the richer. On the ending of prohibition he won the US concession for the sale of Haig and Dewars Whiskeys, and Gordons Gin. But his tireless efforts to amass wealth were not the whole story. He had married Rose, the daughter of a Boston Irish politician,

'Honey Fitz' Fitzgerald and his greatest success was as a father. His nine children, growing up in the light of their father's ambition, were coaxed to develop their many talents to the full, and found themselves, from an early age, dropped in at the deep end of fierce family competition. Joe, the eldest son and his father's favourite, had been to Choate, a private, exclusive, Protestant school and from there to Harvard, where he proved himself to be both a distinguished student and an accomplished athlete. His father was determined that Joe should be as successful in the world of politics. Jack, the second son, attended a Catholic school, perhaps to escape the competitive dominance of his elder brother, and also because his mother, Rose, wanted her children to have a Catholic education. Then he, too, went to Harvard. Joe was proud and dominant. Jack, taking after his mother, was more introspective, but forced himself to compete with the standards set by his elder brother. There were many bitter fights, but their father never interfered, content that Joe, the stronger, should win.

Enraged by their lack of acceptance to polite Boston society, Joseph moved the family to Riverdale, New York, in 1926. Two years later, they bought a large old house in a small village on the coast of the smart playground of Massachusetts, Cape Cod. The village was called Hyannis Port. Then, in 1938, he arrived in London.

Joe and Jack both went to the London School of Economics. Bobby, Jean and Teddy went to London schools, Eunice and Pat went to convent schools in the country and Rosemary, the mentally retarded child who, her father insisted, should stay with the family, remained at home. Kathleen also stayed at the Embassy, to help her mother in her work as Diplomatic hostess.

JPK, compromised because of his closeness to Chamberlain and to the appeasement of Hitler, and horrified by the prospect of American involvement in the war, returned home in 1940.

Despite this, Joe Jr. signed up with the forces on America's entry into the war, and Jack, at first rejected as unfit for service because of his back trouble, took to a strict session of exercises which eventually led to his acceptance by the Navy.

In 1943, Jack's patrol boat in the Solomon Islands was rammed and at first he was reported missing. But he survived and, with ten others, clung to a raft for fifteen hours until they took refuge on a small enemy-held island. For several days and nights the young officer led his men through the jungle. This was the first war action that he or his brother Joe had seen and he had passed through it with honours. Indeed the exploit later became the subject of a film *PT* 109 (financed by his father). It was the first time Jack had achieved something really creditable without the aid of father or family. The first of many blows now struck the Kennedy family. They realised that Rosemary would have to leave them and go into a home. Then, in London, much to the distress of her parents, Kathleen married the son of the Duke of Devonshire—a Protestant. Young Joe, who was then in London, was the only one of the family to lend her support. Just after this a third and far greater calamity struck the family, the first in a sickening succession that was to rob them of four children by violent death. The Kennedys, almost like some cursed, glorious family of ancient mythology, seemed, in their wealth, success and happiness, to attract the lightning of disaster and catastrophe.

Joe, carrying out a dangerous mission off the Belgian coast and piloting a plane filled with explosives, was killed when the aircraft exploded. His body was never found. Joseph Kennedy was shattered and many friends thought he never fully recovered. In his elder son he had placed all his hopes, all his dreams: Joe was to have fulfilled his father's own ambition, of becoming the first Catholic President of the USA. Two weeks after this, Kathleen's husband was killed while leading a raid in France and she retired to an almost monastic life in England.

Back in America, JPK had started on a further episode in his career as a money-maker: he went into real estate. He bought and sold shrewdly, and in Chicago he set up a vast shopping centre—the Merchandise Mart—which to this day is the largest single item in the Kennedy fortune, netting thirteen million dollars a year in rent. Sargent R Shriver, who later married Eunice, was associated with this venture.

Kathleen, nicknamed Kick, did not see the family for many years. At last a rapprochement was made and Kick arranged to spend her summer holiday with her father in the South of France. On a cloudy, rainy night, in the summer of 1948, the chartered plane which was taking her to her father crashed into a mountain, in the Ardeche. At twenty-eight years of age Kathleen Kennedy Cavendish was dead. In the face of such crushing disasters the family, thrown back upon themselves, grew even more united than before.

The Kennedy sisters often remark that it took a long time for any one of the family actually to go out and find non-Kennedys they liked enough to marry. This was particularly true of Jack. Bob had married a girl so like a Kennedy girl as to be almost uncanny. She was small and pretty in a boyish American way, with lively eyes and a firm chin. She was called Ethel Skakel. Within a few years of her marriage she had borne four children—jokingly, she had once said she was determined to beat her mother-in-law's total of nine. Religious to the point of keeping holy water in every room of the house, Ethel was nonetheless adept at coping with pets, children and a busy house—and could play touch-football with the speed and dexterity worthy of a true Kennedy, even when several months pregnant. Devoted to her husband she, of all the Kennedy girls, enjoyed politics most and loved the rough and tumble of the campaigns.

But at thirty-six, Jack was still single. His dates with Jacqueline Bouvier were quite frequent, however, and he would sometimes invite her to dinner parties with his friends and acquaintances in the political sphere.

The Bouviers and the Auchinclosses were not, in any sense, political families. Jackie's step-father, Hugh Dudley Auchincloss, had worked for the Government just prior to the war, but if anything their background was stockbroking; both Jackie's father and step-father were in this profession, as were the majority of Bouviers and Lees. Political discussion was the exception rather than the rule and the Bouviers were regarded as more Republican than Democrat.

Jackie had her first close look at politics when she was sent to ask questions of the new Congressmen on Capitol Hill for the Washington *Times-Herald*, and one of the men she interviewed was her then infrequent beau, Senator John F Kennedy. But as yet Jacqueline Bouvier had not met the Kennedys. Her only contact with politics had been her distant admiration of Adlai Stevenson, the senior statesman of the liberals, the first politician who had made her feel that politics was not simply a sham. He had inspired her. Jackie, like most debutantes, was a completely apolitical animal, but she had an instinct for sincerity.

The young Congressman was her first close look at a politician. Deeply involved with his political career as he was, circumstances dictated that he be in Springfield, Massachusetts, not in the nation's capital where, after the elections, he wished to return wearing a different hat. He was aiming for the Senate. Apart from his father's wishes, Jack Kennedy as Congressman, had had a taste of government and a taste of power, power as it could be used for the good of, for the betterment of the United States. His money, the vast millions, was often criticised, but without this money his life might have been very different. The financial burden of the political campaigns is so vast that it is still well nigh impossible for a man without money to become President. His family, too, were jibed at for the sheer size of their numbers. But without the security of this family, large enough to look after both each other and the complications of the family business affairs, he would have had family burdens to carry as well as political ones. And just at this moment in his career he had no need of a wife. He was well aware, however, that if the country were to take him to its heart in a big way, a spouse should be found.

He already had plenty of ladies to help in the campaign— three sisters at the ready, Pat, Eunice and Jean and an equally enthusiastic sister-in-law, Ethel. His mother, Rose, also gave him her support and there were also his brothers, Bobby and Ted. The family was dedicated to conquering the state of Massachusetts.

Jack's courtship of the young journalist started very slowly. Sometimes they would visit friends for dinner or take in a film. They avoided political parties that abounded in Washington; he, because he lived and breathed politics all day and was trying to sit back on his image as the gay, young, bachelor Congressman, and she, because she did not like them. But she did go up to the Capitol. One of the inconsequential stories the paper wanted her to do was interview the pages at the Senate on their views on the Senators. She also asked two Congressmen, Richard Nixon and John Kennedy their views on the pages. Mr Nixon gave a predictably serious, considered response. 'Those pages,' he said 'could have great political futures; they are so clever and have such experience.' Kennedy's answer was humorous and sarcastic—and must have appealed to the young reporter—the pages and the Senators, he suggested, should change places. Frequently she contrived to be there at lunch time and they would go and have a hamburger together. Eventually he took her home to meet his family at Hyannis Port—and they became engaged to get engaged! They avoided being seen around the capital where gossip seemed to grow on the trees in the squares, spreading faster than telegraph cables. They would often go to their friends, the Bartletts, and play *Monopoly*. Appropriately enough, Jack was often the winner.

She would take him to galleries. He preferred seascapes. But there were many interests they had in common. He would ask her to translate such political works as those by de Gaulle, or books on that part of Indo-China now known as Vietnam. For Jackie it was a political education. So gradually they grew together.

Jack, in many ways so very like her father, impressed Jacqueline with his intelligence and style. He was her senior by twelve years and had been quite a Don Juan in his youth— never something he had attempted to conceal—and he was surrounded by an aura of excitement of intelligence. While Jacqueline certainly knew much more than he about history and the arts, in his eyes this merely made her more interesting —but she was not in his class as far as brains were concerned. John F Kennedy was later thought to understand women not at all; he was not a man with time to spare for romantic interludes. In the bright light of his senatorial youth, he was a man whom she could respect.

They shared one passion, poetry. She, who could always learn poems fast, learnt his favourite ones and he loved her to repeat them to him. When they could, they went to the theatre. They both also liked classical music. Jackie's favourites were Brahms and Berlioz and Jack's Beethoven and Sibelius; in later years he would keep a hi-fi set in his bedroom. Impossible to realise, in these early days, how much of his future life would be a battleground for her and how much she would be called upon to sacrifice.

Their courting was slow, some might even think rather unromantic. Jack Kennedy, having hung on to his bachelor-hood all this time, was in no hurry for marriage. Time passed and they did, at any rate, fall in love and become engaged. Those closest to them knew before the official announcement came—their families would have been horrified if the news had broken when they opened their morning papers. Already political reasons started edging into Jacqueline Bouvier's life.

The large circulation *Saturday Evening Post* was doing an article on the Senator from Massachusetts, its cover line 'Jack Kennedy—the Senate's Gay Young Bachelor'. The engagement had to be postponed, so as not to spoil the magazine copyline. But Jackie, happy, did not stop to think really hard how much the political world was going to intrude. A Senator's job was rather like that of a top executive and she was, she determined, going to be the very best sort of helpful wife.

Her fiancé gave her an emerald ring, the twin green stones each surrounded by diamonds. Jackie and her mother raced round making preparations. As at her coming out party Jackie, hating an ostentatious show, decided that Hammersmith Farm at Newport, her parents' summer house, would be the simplest and most beautiful for the reception—especially just before harvest. The wedding date was thus set for 12 September, the ceremony to take place at the nearby St Mary's, a Catholic church with particularly beautiful old stained glass windows.

On the eve of the wedding the bride and groom attended a bridal party, given by Mr and Mrs Auchincloss at the Clambake Club, Newport, Rhode Island, and the scene of Jackie's deb dance many years before. Here the family and friends, the fourteen ushers and ten bridesmaids old enough to attend, were regaled with speeches by the bride and groom-to-be. Jack Kennedy, in a relaxed and witty speech, as relaxed as those he gave to his voting public, declared his real reason for marriage to be fear! Fear that his fiancée, in her capacity as a journalist, could menace his career. She, as an Inquiring Camera Girl, he said, was just getting too inquisitive. What else was there to do but marry the girl and remove her from her dangerous position! Jackie, who had by then left her post on the Washington *Times-Herald* never to return, was not to be outdone. Saying that her mother had always advised her that a suitor's letters were a good test of his ardour, she held up the one obviously cherished card she had received from him. It simply read, 'Wish you were here, Jack'. This original legend was on the back of a colour postcard sent from Bermuda.

The bridal dinner had been the culmination in virtually a week of celebration before the wedding, which was to be a big one. Five days before that the Kennedys had put on their own show at Hyannis Port. Joe, obviously delighted with his son's choice, entertained the whole bridal party, the Auchinclosses, the ushers and the bridesmaids. The party took on Kennedy style, with a hectic routine of touch-football, charades— Jackie was an excellent actress—and short excursions on the boat *Victura*. Jackie was no great sailor. A delightful picture of them both on the boat, in shorts and tough, pocketed shirts in a hair-ruffling breeze, appeared on a magazine cover when they announced their engagement and, when asked how it had been taken, Jackie replied that her husband had the passion for sailing. She had only stayed in that boat long enough for the picture to be taken. There was the fun of Joseph Kennedy's birthday, when each of his children gave him a sweater as a joke present, and insisted on putting one on top of the other. The party was a gay one. They welcomed the new member warmly into the family.

The families finally assembled on the day of the marriage. Saturday, 12 September, 1953 could not have been a more perfect day. A distinguished congregation awaited Jackie's arrival in a church decorated with a profusion of pink and white flowers, chosen by the bride, and arranged in large tapering sprays.

Jacqueline entered the church, her face unveiled and her large eyes shining. Her skin was lightly tanned, her hair, full and curly, had been touched by the sun and clung in tendrils round her ears. A lace veil, lent by her grandmother, Mrs James T Lee, patterned with large roses and held in place by orange blossom at the nape of the neck, swooped down to a wide float and spread across six feet of the aisle.

The dress, made in creamy white faille to blend with the

veil, had been made locally. It was slim-waisted, with a hundred folds crossing the bodice and covering the whole dress above the waist. It had neat cap sleeves, and a widely flaring skirt—its fullness supported by several ruffling petticoats. Beautifully edged in frills, the skirt was trimmed with wide rosettes, the centre of each being garlanded with orange blossom. Round her neck she wore a single string of pearls, and on her left arm a diamond bracelet, her wedding present from Jack. She carried a bouquet of orchids and lilies.

The bridesmaids, in long pink taffeta dresses sashed in deep aubergine and trimmed with frills at the neck, also wore a single string of pearls. Lee, as sister of the bride, was matron-of-honour and wore a dress similar to those of the other bridesmaids, but of a deeper pink. The shoulders were cut wide, in the fashion of the Fifties, and the long sashes hung down almost to the hems. They all wore short white gloves like the bride's and carried bouquets of roses and carnations. Each one received a silver photograph frame as a bridesmaid's present. Janet, Jackie's nine year old half-sister, was also a bridesmaid and her half-brother Jamie, then aged six and dressed in a frilled white shirt and black velvet shorts, acted as a page.

Jack Kennedy, handsome and at that time so slender as to look, according to some more maternal voters, 'as if he needed a square meal', stood awaiting her at the altar, with Cardinal Cushing, who was to marry them. And as Jackie approached, the wedding ceremony began.

Outside, the sun shone and the spectators waited. The ceremony over, the new Mr and Mrs John Fitzgerald Francis Kennedy emerged, the wind pulling at the bride's hair and veil, and the sun dazzling their eyes. But both their smiles were joyful.

A glittering cavalcade, they all set off for the farm. There, at hundreds of small round tables, they had lunch on the lawn, a lunch of champagne and pineapple and a wedding cake in four

c

tiers with icing 'waves' topped with tiny roses. And later the twelve hundred guests, led by Jackie and Jack Kennedy, danced to Meyer Davis's orchestra, the same that had played at her mother's wedding. In the background the fields were filled with ripening corn, the trees just beginning to be tinged with autumn colour. At last the new Mrs Kennedy mounted the old staircase, stood by the turn of the stair near the antique mirror and the grandfather clock and held her bouquet aloft. She slowly smiled, and let the flowers fall and vanished forever as a Bouvier. Her day as a Kennedy bride was over.

Chapter 4

LADIES AND GENTLEMEN, YOUR PRESIDENT

On their return from their honeymoon in Acapulco, the young Senator and his wife moved into their new house. It was one of several they were to rent, or loan from parents during the early years. There was never time to settle, their travels would not have allowed it—there was always somewhere to go—a session of speeches, Europe. There was more unpacking and packing to do in that year than she had ever done before. Luckily, they were not yet at the stage of needing a permanent home base. But for the neat, quiet, well-dressed Jackie it must have been maddening at times. Not all her clothes could be transported and sometimes the very thing she wanted would be at the other end of the country. She eventually, because she had to, encapsulated her wardrobe and cut down the number of colours. Many of her accessories were now planned to go with everything and selection of an outfit became both easier and much faster.

When the winter came, Jackie, not wanting to become a mere housewife, a dread that remained from her schooldays at Miss Porter's, took the opportunity of going back to college. Her husband was due at the Senate every day, so she reported to the Georgetown School of Foreign Service; her subject, American History. For one so well versed in European, particularly French, history, her information was rather hazy about that of her own country, which she was crossing and re-crossing whilst accompanying her Senator husband on his speech-making tours. Jack himself knew a lot about the subject and she, knowing his boredom with the mediocre, was afraid that if she were unable to discuss knowledgeably those things with which he was so much concerned, she would soon be categorised as such herself.

She approached her studies with concentration and, while her beloved European history was in some ways more subtle and complex than the wars of the New Frontiers, she soon became well acquainted with the luminaries of American History—so often quoted by her husband in his speeches—such as Jefferson and Lincoln. Meanwhile she learned about those speeches and about the Boston, Massachusetts background of her husband. Her homes, all of them, were the frequent haunt of Jack's political friends and colleagues. Even the conversation of her brother and sister-in-law would centre on votes, voters and the wider issues of the political world with which they were all so much involved. Jackie soon discovered that, unlike Ethel, she had basically no interest either in the complex voting percentages that could swing a State, or in the political machinery that governed them; nor was she so much prepared to like the tough political professionals with whom her husband spent so much of his time. Even her husband's speeches, several of which often had to be delivered in a day, and which, as a result, were often repeated more than once, would frequently find her staring into the middle distance. Her husband's politics interested her as far as he himself was concerned, but the minute they turned to abstract topics of conversation in which her husband eagerly participated, she would long for evenings over dinner with the Auchinclosses, where the conversation might have centered light-heartedly on the latest play or book. She had very definite tastes on the style in which she liked to live. She liked French food, being very much against the American tendency towards tasteless cooking. Unlike many Americans who keep artificial flowers, she liked fresh ones, in spite of the fact that they died quickly in the dry atmosphere of the central heating. She would arrange them in masses in copper pots, to create what looked like a bright single poppy-head of colour. She also started to inject good sense into the Senator's round, trying to ensure that he relaxed when he came back from Capitol Hill. Jack who, like all bachelors, had led a somewhat irregular life before settling down, appreciated her care.

Eighteen months after the wedding, in 1955, Jackie realised she was pregnant. The Kennedys had always gone in for big families, Bobby already had four children, and Jack himself was one of nine—but sadly, she miscarried. It was also a time of political trial. In the summer of 1956 Jack was put forward in the race for the Vice Presidential nomination for the Democrats. The Presidential candidate was Adlai Stevenson, who was running against the incumbent Dwight D Eisenhower. For Jack, the race was against Estes Kefauver, and was one that his father warned him not to run. Jack narrowly lost and this first political setback hit him hard. Politics, the greatest single enthusiasm of his life, was capable of precipitating him into moments of terrible despair. He left Jackie, not particularly well in the last few months of her second pregnancy, and hastened for comfort and advice to his father who was taking his usual holiday in the South of France. It was here, basking in the Mediterranean sun and recovering from his disappointment, that he received a telephone call from his in-laws at Newport: Jackie had again lost the baby, a girl, and had under gone an operation. Shocked, he immediately flew back to be with her. Two weeks later he left to campaign for the Democrat nominee, Stevenson, putting his defeat behind him and fixing his hopes constantly on 1960. Jackie, in the face of her second loss, could only hope and pray that next time she too would have better luck. Meanwhile their lives continued very much the same as before, with trips to Hyannis Port to be with the Kennedys, visits to Merrywood and Newport and the frequent separations brought about by vital campaigning. Stevenson had lost, and the Democrats were working hard.

In 1957 Jackie was to know what it was like to be public property. Neither President Eisenhower nor indeed his

Vice President, Richard Milhous Nixon, had a sliver of news value; both of them had been around too long. But the newspapers, the magazines and the press in general had been quick to note the attractiveness of the failed Vice-Presidential candidate in Chicago, whose looks and casual sense of style, added up to good news—as did his wife. They were the darlings of the press, and articles on the rest of the clan, as it almost came to be known, abounded. Articles on the Senator's wife appeared in all the women's magazines. Her trips to France had this time steered her away from *les jeunes*, the cheap cafés of the Left Bank and the student bookshops to the haute couture salons of the Faubourg St. Honoré on the Right Bank. There she would sit on their elegant sofas and select clothes for herself, encouraged by her mother-in-law, Rose, who herself had patronised the French houses heavily since her time as wife of the Ambassador of the United States in England, selecting a silver and white Molyneux dress for her presentation to King George VI and Queen Elizabeth. Jackie bought mostly from Givenchy, Balenciaga and Cardin. Givenchy was her favourite and she his. The house delighted in creating clothes for her, her figure being rangy and model-like, her taste exquisitely simple. Givenchy himself has described her as 'the perfect customer' and has even designed some of his classic clothes exclusively for her, a rare honour indeed. Often the house would, with the dresses sent from France, add a suggested list of accessories. These would be photographed, and Jackie could order them if she wished. Instead of her close-fitting Paris clothes, however, she would swathe herself in maternity smocks. In 1957, hoping desperately for a child, she again ordered the maternity smocks out of the cupboard, and bought Paris copies from the New York Departmental Stores to suit her new figure.

Resting at home this time, to be sure of the baby, Jackie watched as the so-called Kennedy machine took final shape. Many of the Kennedy machine were family, Bobby, latterly

Teddy and the willing brothers-in-law, Sargent Shriver and Steven Smith. There was also Kenny O'Donnell, a slight, dark-haired man of Irish descent but untypically taciturn, who had been a contemporary of Robert Kennedy's at Harvard. Lawrence O'Brien was another—another Irishman who, with the Kennedys, provoked the nickname of the Irish mafia. The same age as Jack but heavier in build, he was never to be ruffled or panicked—it was Larry and Ken, Larry the super-calm organizer and Ken the tactician.

Then there were the others, Sorensen, Theodore H Sorensen, young and handsome, an intellectual, he was an ideas man for Jack Kennedy—they thought ideas together, they wrote speeches almost together and Sorensen particularly, a determined liberal, was to point the way for the candidate. Louis Harris, ebullient, well versed in his special sphere and in his thirties already the proprietor of a poll-taking organization which was to comb the country countless times, was also a member; the press and publicity man was Pierre Salinger, round-faced, dark eyed, practical and funny, he quickly endeared himself to the nation's press. There were others, many others, but this was the core and Jackie Kennedy could, after 1956, expect them, together, or in groups, to be surrounding her husband, especially at Hyannis Port where her father-in-law who had so many enemies he could not publicly join the campaign, was able to join in.

At last they had bought a home in McLean, Virginia, not too far from Merrywood. It was a big house on Hickory Hill, with pleasant, spacious rooms and large grounds, including a big garden filled with big old oak trees, a perfect place for children. They had already lost two children, the house was at least a twenty minute drive for the Senator each morning to his office and the emptiness was a constant reminder of their sad childlessness. Luckily, in 1955 Bobby was looking for a house large enough for his family. At thirty years old he was the father of three sons and a daughter. Reluctantly, Jack and

Jackie sold him their house, and themselves looked for something more central and less large.

In the summer of 1957, the again pregnant Jackie and her husband started a real look for another house. This time they were lucky, there was a house on N Street West Georgetown, the Belgravia of Washington, where Jackie had visited as a deb. With its pleasant old facade, well proportioned rooms, and large windows, it was very much like the Georgian terrace houses of London. Jackie remembered it well, and when it came up for sale, she was ecstatic. They bought it immediately, for seventy thousand dollars. She began to assemble furniture and again, but this time tentatively, prepared a nursery. She was going to use the same pretty wicker bassinet used for herself and Lee as children but instead of the original delicate pink *point d'esprit*, she trimmed it with a more practical white cotton broderie anglaise.

On 28 November of that year, the day after Thanksgiving, Jackie was taken to hospital, the New York Hospital which had been alerted to the likelihood of a difficult birth. There, by Caesarian section, a daughter was born. At last they had their child, and they called her Caroline. After she was born, they took her home to their apartment on Park Avenue, soon to be replaced by the new house in the capital. Jack already had to stay there most of the time as he had to sit in the Senate. His wife had been apart from him much of the time she was pregnant, her physician and his department being alerted for her confinement in New York. They both looked forward to the move. The house on N Street had at last been completed, Jackie's sister Lee, then Mrs Lee Canfield of New York, overseeing the final touches. This was the house Jackie was to love more than any other, of which she said 'I love our home in Washington. There has always been a child in it. Caroline was three weeks old when we moved into our home in Georgetown. My sweet little house leans slightly to one side and the stairs creak.'

Number 3307 N Street could hardly be called a slum. It was in the smartest part of Washington, around which a bevy of politicians lived. The house was furnished in a style appropriate to the beautiful old fashioned facade. Jackie, never a lover of pop art and perspex, loved antique furniture, some of which she imported from France and England. The rooms were full of books in bookshelves built from floor to ceiling. There were paintings, many of them seascapes, her husband's favourite, and low tables with large pots of flowers. The walls were a pale pink, the sofas upholstered in pastel green. For the Kennedy brothers and sisters this was very different from their own rough and tumble households, which were also beautifully furnished, but more in the traditional American style.

The dining room on the ground floor had silver candlesticks on the oval table, antique cane chairs and gold side lamps over an antique sideboard. It was to become an elegant meeting place for politicians and bright young Washington society. Jackie, whose love of politics diminished as her acquaintance with it increased, did at last realise and accept the full importance of these things for her husband, developing her own interests with new friends among the women involved, like herself, on the periphery of the political world.

The house, though old, was designed with typical American efficiency. The dining room on the ground floor was close to the reception room, and big enough to cope with a large party. On the whole, however, the Kennedys preferred small dinner parties, often sprinkled with their relatives. The kitchen and pantry, both roomy and well equipped, were also on this floor. The bedrooms were on the first floor, a double room with a bathroom each for the Senator and his wife and two spare bedrooms also with bathrooms, the walls hung with paintings framed in gold. Upstairs on the third floor was the nursery and the room for the nanny, Maud Shaw. Caroline's room was palest pink, a favourite colour of Jacqueline's, with an edging of red roses round the wall, the furniture being painted white and trimmed with small pink leaves. The curtains were white organdie trimmed with pink and the carpet was white stretching through to the nanny's room.

Caroline, or Buttons as her father called her, was to grow up feminine and reserved, rather like her mother. Her parents called her Caroline for many reasons. Jack's reputedly favourite book was Lord David Cecil's book about Lord Melbourne, the witty, sardonic, gay Prime Minister of nineteenth century England, in which there were many women called Caroline. Jackie's sister had been named Caroline Lee, but her sharp, astringent personality toned better with her middle name than the gentler Caroline. It was also the name of a distinguished Bouvier forbear. The John F Kennedys seemed at last to have found the peace, rest and happiness they had wanted. The separations they had undergone were rumoured for several years to be a sign of unhappiness but it was a struggling, fine marriage between two strong-minded people. Jack, a bachelor until his thirty-sixth year, did find it took time to adjust to one base, one wife. Jackie, expecting a slower, more refined style of life, found it hard to accustom herself to the publicity and restrictions of a political role. She was, in many ways, a socialite. On her marriage, as a girl with some sophistication and a good mind, she was thrown into something she did not expect and did not really want. Loving this handsome Senator, perhaps she closed her eyes to her probable future—which must have been very evident to anyone acquainted with the Kennedy family—only to have them forcibly opened later. The love was there but it was not all roses.

Caroline's birth was to bring them closer together, and Jackie, having successfully given birth, was able, once more, to pursue her own life. She spent much time with her sister, the gay Lee, now divorced, who introduced her sister to the 'Beautiful People' of New York, the smart set who lived a life of fun and ease. Meanwhile, the Senator moved slowly along the road to the Presidency. His small coterie of helpers appeared more and more around the oval table at the Georgetown house. He and his brother became known to the top political organisers around the entire country, the men whose telephone dials could pull votes. These were the men to explain to, to talk to, to become enrolled in the Kennedy bandwagon in 1960. 'The men in the silk suits in smoke-filled rooms' as they were known, were the political fixers and party machine boys whose support meant the difference between success and failure. Their knowledge of the dilettante world of New York was slight.

In New York, the art galleries were constantly discovering new artists, there were plays (there are no theatres in Washington), there were dinner parties where witty gossip and fascinating conversation both flourished. In Washington the political parties were of a uniform pattern. The guests would assemble, there would be cocktails and general talk, then there would be dinner, after which strict segregation would take place. The men would stay with the men, pulling out cigars— Jack Kennedy liked Havanas—discussing their favourite burning topic, always political. The women would stay with the women. If she was lucky, they might be interested in something other than children, maids, shopping and money. Jackie loved children—'If you bungle raising your children,' she once said, 'I don't think whatever else you do will matter very much'—but she was not a woman's woman, preferring the company of men. Apart from Toni Bradlee, Bunny Mellon and her sister Lee, she does not have that many close girl friends. The Washington parties, unless one hurled oneself into the political scene, and did not object to being always on guard against giving offence, tended to be monotonous and desperately predictable.

Campaigning came by way of a relief. Jackie joined her husband on many of these storms through the sleepy New England towns. Her first marathon was in 1958. The Senator, who was seeking a second term, won with a colossal majority.

She gave him all the help she could, becoming aware for
perhaps the first time of what her husband was putting into his
quest for leadership. When they had campaigned in the early
days of their marriage, she had taken it much slower, and she
was still new to it, excited by it. She felt she had married a
'Whirlwind'. Later she said 'not many people know how
physically wearing such a campaign' (as the one in 1958) 'can
be. Some mornings you're up at seven, and you visit a dozen
towns during the day. You shake hundreds of hands in the
afternoon and hundreds more at night. You get so tired you
catch yourself laughing and crying at the same time. But you
pace yourself and you get through it. You just look at it as
something you have to do. You knew it would come, and you
knew it was worth it.'

She did, to some extent, find such campaigning exhilarating,
in spite of her general attitude of resignation. Between her time
looking after their baby and the campaign, their life was
divided between Christmas at Palm Beach, Florida, at the
home of the Kennedy parents, much of the summer spent at
Hyannis Port at their own house, a few yards away from those
of Joseph Kennedy and Robert Kennedy, while the rest of the
year was spent in Washington. The life that Jacqueline Bouvier
expected vanished in the wind.

However, left a lot to her own devices, she did establish the
style for which she was to become known. Apart from her
great love of eighteenth century France reflected in the
furnishings of the Georgetown house and later the Hyannis
Port summer cottage, she struck out on her own for a great
many other things. Her clothes now nearly all came from
couturiers, though she was not above buying skin-tight
trousers and simple gingham dresses off the peg. Her clothes
were later to become the centre of a furore when criticised for
their cost. She replied they could hardly cost *that* much unless
she wore sable underwear! During the fifties, known for their
fol-de-rols, heart-shaped necklines, full skirts and general

fuss, Jackie developed a style of sophisticated simplicity. She abandoned her experiment with the short, layered Italian hairstyle which had never suited her rather austere features very well and now wore her hair smooth and bouffant to just above the ears. She was particularly fond of earrings and found, like many women with strong jaw-lines, that they pull attention away from the jaw. Her favourites were Chanel-style ones, a pearl surrounded by three stones on a banding of gold. Her accessories were the best. Hermes and Gucci bags, the snob symbols of millions of women who can really afford them, really suit her. Of hats, she made the pill box a fashion classic. When she later had to be hatted, this was the style she most often chose, having them made up in the same fabric as her favourite coats and suits. When very cold she would wear a mink, but unless the temperature were freezing, she more often wore correct cloth fabric coats. For evening occasions she would wear long ball gowns made with matching jackets, or a satin short coat over a cocktail dress. Her jewellery, too, was stunning yet simple, drop earrings and simple matching necklaces and often her bridal present, the diamond bracelet, would be the most she would wear, looking starkly simple next to more ostentatious political wives. She was a follower of the little black dress. Shops in New York would know she was a fussy dresser for, having bought clothes in the French capital, she had a professional's eye for cut, and quality. Off-the-peg America could not entrance her, though she did, very occasionally, patronize a few of her home-grown couturiers. She favoured simple shapes, and would sometimes plump for a single colour, like a long red velvet dress, lightened only by her rings and some earrings.

Her sports were also the ladylike sports. Having once broken her ankle at the Kennedy game of touch-football she gave it up. She had never seemed able to master it and she once asked what exactly she was supposed to do, having got the ball. Instead, she loved to ride alone and grew fond, under her husband's tutelage, of sailing. She taught her daughter to ride as soon as she could and acquired for her a pony called Macaroni. Before the little girl could sit on a horse she bought a trap, similar to the one she had ridden in to a Virginian tercentenary, in which she would take Caroline for rides. This smacked of the aristocracy to some of the President's advisers. They were worried about her during the forthcoming campaign. Her voice, always quiet, seemed to become breathless and husky in public. Shy, she never liked to shout and the days of the campaign were so long that she held her voice down in restraint so that it should last. Her husband, always scared of his voice going, drank at least a pint of milk a day.

She was certainly nobody's idea of a homebody, all-American, rootin'-tootin' political wife, doling out the stickers, the banners, laughing with the boys, being one of the girls. She always had that air of elusiveness and mystique bred in her by her father. Sometimes the rooms full of noise, smoke and confusion would seem frightening. She would stand slightly aside and automatically withdraw. Unlike her husband in this way, she did not find it easy to come forward to the people. No-one does or ever will know who was the more relieved, when it became obvious, in the late spring of 1960, that the possible Presidential candidate's wife would not be able to attend the campaigning—the wife herself or the President's counsellors. Jackie was again pregnant.

In the ugly political world that erupts before a Presidential candidate is chosen, even the simplicity of this backfired. Rumour had it that it was a deliberate ruse to gain sympathy and support for Jack Kennedy, whose machine by now was being spoken of as a juggernaut, instead of the efficient organisation it actually was. Other rumours suggested that Jackie had become pregnant only because the political advisers hesitated to put her on the campaign stand. And finally, because of Jackie's understandable non-attendance, particularly

at some of the most rigorous campaign tours, the rumours even
flew that the marriage was breaking up and that Joseph
Kennedy had offered his daughter-in-law a million dollars to
stay with his son so as not to spoil his chances.

Both the Kennedys, their natural longing for privacy often
mistaken for arrogance, received this buffeting badly and
with shock. Their separations were bad enough, the pregnancy
on her part and the campaign on his were tiring enough,
without this. They decided to take as little notice as possible.
Jackie attended the speeches and visits she had always meant to
attend, doing everything in her power to appeal to the voters.
Jack did not mention his wife's condition once in an effort to
dampen the whole thing down. The American women who
drew up to watch him in large numbers whenever he spoke
thought his silence the worst indictment and only when he
realised this did he mention it. Theodore H White's book
The Making of the President explains how it grew to be a matter
Jack Kennedy mentioned finally, affectionately but with
defiance, to put pay to the malicious gossip which threatened
the happiness of the event. One noon in Oregon impulsively he
offered the courteous excuse that his wife was absent because
she was 'otherwise committed'—later on the quote changed to
a definitive, 'My wife is going to have a boy in November.'
When asked how he knew it would be a boy, he retorted that
his wife had told him. Their longing for a son was very
obvious and their luck in this, and much else that year, held.
Before John Fitzgerald Junior was born the campaign had two
stages further to go. Los Angeles and the Democratic convention where a Presidential candidate was to be selected, and
then the final countdown on 9 November.

Los Angeles, the sprawling motorway-webbed Californian
metropolis, played host to the Democrats in 1960. There
John F Kennedy, one of the four contestants for the world's
most powerful office, stayed in a hideaway on North Rossmore
Boulevard, accompanied by a single close friend, Dave Powers,

his friend and jokester. Jackie, scared of the crowds, knowing that she had done her work and that she would have no influence on dyed-in-the-wool political leaders and fixers, stayed at home waiting for the news. She felt that in her condition she could do no more. During the Primaries she had accompanied her husband early on and had penned thousands of letters to Kennedy workers all over the country. She helped make a film with him to show at the Convention, she wrote a news sheet column called *Campaign Wife* that went to the Kennedy workers everywhere. She met with women leaders and discussed everything with them from babies to politics; she even went on television several times.

They both waited, he in his hide-out, she in Hyannis Port. A victim of growing nervousness she tried to dabble away with her paints. As if willing him to win, she painted a picture of him in a splendid admiral's hat, returning to the house on a flotilla via the sea, while she and Caroline on the jetty waved to him. Of the success of this gift to him no-one knows, except that after he had received it, when asked what he would give his wife for her next birthday, he said wryly that he was painting it—that evening! Even the sight of the crowd was too much for her. Eventually he telephoned her, after she and all the world knew that Wyoming had swung it for him. At last they were both able to relax. They both addressed the press the next day, Jackie accompanied by her mother and step-father, Jack alone.

They were reunited only after he had finished his business in the Convention town, to choose his Vice-Presidential running mate. He chose Lyndon Baines Johnson. Then the race against Nixon, the Republican Candidate, was on, with trips up and down the country and little time to relax at home. It was an uphill fight. Although Jack Kennedy the good looking Senator had been featured by the magazines, the newspapers had featured his opponent, who was aided by the stable hand of help from an old President. Richard Milhous Nixon was the protégé of President Eisenhower, who was, after all, still sitting in the seat of power.

The house at Hyannis Port became a centre for strange men on the telephone, strange men in the rooms, press men outside the house barely a few feet away, press conferences at Bobby's house. Jackie Kennedy never knew whom she would meet at breakfast, nor who would still be there for a last drink at night. The house was no longer her own. By now quite obviously pregnant, she would try unobtrusively to escape them all, and go for as many unphotographed walks as possible with her daughter. The baby was expected at Christmas, and they had early decided to name him after his father. Caroline was almost the same age as Jackie herself had been when she had become an elder sister and her mother described the baby as a wonderful Christmas gift for her daughter. She compared the new baby to Raggity-Annie, Caroline's favourite doll, a rag doll with round eyes and woollen hair. Caroline soon got used to the idea and also accustomed herself more readily than her mother to the strangeness of their invaded home. Her father was rarely to be seen and even Jackie managed to keep up with him only by seeing him off whenever he left, often very early in the morning, on a whistle-stop tour. Wearing an old raincoat, a headscarf round her head, she would fondly kiss him goodbye, no matter what the weather was, no matter what the time. The summer and autumn wore on and on. She acceded to the many requests for interviews and the papers became saturated with her wide-faced smile. Articles on her clothes, her house, her interests abounded.

Eventually the election day came. The Hyannis Port compound was turned into a seething Kennedy control centre. The Senator had at last returned home. The brother-in-law campaign manager and his ebullient wife never rested—their house was a mass of cables, telephones, sandwiches made in a rush, cokes and people. Apart from the family and the helpers, there were old friends, friends from the press . . . and outside the newspaper men who would circle like vultures, waiting for the news of the night. Jack went to and from these houses, while Jackie, a little apart as always, entertained their friends, the William Waltons. The politics discussed at dinner that evening were unusually relaxed. The tension started with the television screen. At ten-thirty, when Jackie thought the President was surely the man sitting beside her, she quietly acknowledged his victory, calling him Bunny, her pet name for him. He, still tense, was not sure. Eventually he sent her off to bed—the two lost children still weighed heavily on their minds—and he left the house for the last time as Senator. He went to Bobby's house and there he stayed until sure of victory. The votes were still coming in, but they had been sure he would win the election since about midnight. Early the next morning, still waiting for his opponent to concede defeat, the future President walked with his daughter on the beach. Later, he watched Richard Nixon's concession of defeat on television with closeness and the relief of 'There but for the Grace of God go I', glad it was not him at the Ambassadors Hotel, Los Angeles, rather embarrassed at the sadness of Pat Nixon's tearful face. Jackie was out walking when he went to look for her. A solitary figure in an old baggy raincoat, looking at the sea. He went up to her on the beach. He had what he wanted, both from the country and from her, and now she would be with him during the Presidency. They slowly walked back to the house. She would have to change for photographs and a trip to the Hyannis Port Armoury. The nation was waiting for them. For the first time in cavalcade, they drove up to the Armoury. The crowd applauded, flash bulbs shone. Elbowing their way through, they managed to enter. There was a hush and then the announcement, 'Ladies and Gentlemen: Your President.'

Chapter 5

AT THE COURT OF KING JOHN

THE day of the Inauguration was a snowy one. They came to the nation like a young Ice King and Queen, arriving in a cavalcade of cars and distinguished attendants. America was full of excited anticipation, knowing that something special was happening . . . the articles on the Senator, then the President-elect, had not been in vain. In the first car sat President Eisenhower, distinguished old general, his face lined from long service in the field of combat, both in the war and in politics, balding and rather thin. Next to him, Jack Kennedy, young and full of vitality, his face lined only from a sharp wind off Cape Cod and smiles of happy years with the State of Massachusetts. Behind, the contrast was even greater. Mrs Eisenhower's small, heart-shaped face, brown hair curling into the famous fringe, next to Jacqueline's almost leonine beauty. One already a grandmother, her companion a young mother—a little shy of the crowds but encouraged by the older woman to wave and smile in answer to their welcome. She was thirty-one, the third youngest First Lady in all the history of America. Men in top hats and their fur-swathed ladies stood on the balcony. The faces below cheered the new arrivals. Jack Kennedy's formal attire only made his youth more pronounced. Jacqueline, in a simple beige coat trimmed with sable, a matching hat far at the back of her head, looked elegant and rather delicate against the bulky furs of the other women. Looking around she could see that her husband's family were here in force and that her sister-in-law Ethel's face was streaked with tears.

The ceremony of transferring the greatest power in the world began. The new President was cool and calm. Holding

the family Bible beneath his hand he made the oath; then, to
the expectant crowds below him, he delivered his first presidential speech. The New Frontier had been declared but the
real battle had yet to be joined.

Already, however, the barriers were down for the new
First Lady. When she appeared that evening to attend the five
Inaugural balls, the crowd had already identified a star. The
car that carried her was brightly lit inside. The sound was
heard for the first time, 'Jackieee, Jackieeeee'. They attended
the balls together, the President in white tie and tails, and his
wife in a dress of white *peau d'ange*. She had designed the outfit
herself, and it had been made for her by her dressmaker. The
dress itself was a close fitting sheath with a jewelled bodice, and
a chiffon overblouse. Her cape, also of *peau d'ange*, was covered
in white chiffon, had a high collar which covered the round
collar of the dress beneath and fell to the ground behind her
like a train. Her hair had been dressed for the occasion by
Kenneth, her hair dresser, and was swept back high off her forehead to show beautiful drop earrings. Amid the white snow she
shone like an icicle star. Her husband, crossed and re-crossed
the town with her to the Inaugurals. There were five, but those
at the last two were to be disappointed. Recuperating from the
birth of their second child, and still unused to the hectic life of
a public person, she returned to the White House.

Her husband, his colleagues, brothers and others in the
Presidential retinue continued until four o'clock. Frank
Sinatra, friend of the President's actor brother-in-law, Peter
Lawford, had arranged a gala and the President's father, who
had dreamed of this night for too many years to count, threw a
party at a Washington restaurant. At length Secret Service
agents accompanied him to the columns of the White House.
He crept quietly through his bedroom door. The Kennedys
had arrived.

Now Jackie had to get used to living in the middle of
politics. She still could not admit to liking the subject, but it

proved less unpleasant than she had imagined. Her husband, installed in the seat of power, was there not only metaphorically but physically. As President he had to remain more static than he had been as a Senator and had himself jokingly remarked how conveniently near his home his office was. Much of his time was taken up in meetings and conferences, but at least now they were together. The children had breakfast with him and, occasionally, Jackie would have lunch with him. The separation of the old days had thrown her very much onto her own resources and there had been days when Jack would return from the fray utterly exhausted, when she would worry. Since her marriage she had become a great worrier, feeling that perhaps she was not able to cope adequately and disturbed by her husband's frequent inability to conceal his eagerness to return to the field of battle.

For their first year the two had been close; now during the time she had dreaded most, their marriage really bloomed again. He suddenly realized she was not just the beautiful wife, a slight liability who was thought light-weight by his political friends, aloof by the public and averse to spending hours with his family. She had never been and flatly announced that she would never be a committee woman. Jackie, with age, still had not become a woman's woman. Not that she was unfriendly—during her school days at Miss Porter's, she had had many friends—but she had never been a cosy chatterer and now, surrounded by the formality of the White House and the constant public attention attendant on her new role, she treasured her privacy even more highly than before. Although fond of young people, she could not conceive of herself running a nation-wide Girl Guide movement nor even the newly formed Peace Corps. Neither of these gave scope to her real interest in life—to be and to appear to be creative and artistic. She realized, however, as she walked through the White House, on a conducted tour given her by Mamie Eisenhower a few short weeks before she entered the house of which she was to be mistress herself, there was something she could do.

The White House, built on the proportions of a small palace, had become, during the succession of its many inhabitants, a shamble of disorganisation at every level. The taste of some previous presidential occupants, all of whom had been able to change the decor during their tenure, had been horrendous. The furniture had changed from President to President, and previous First Ladies had felt no compunction about selling off some of the older items to make way for more modern ones. The result was a hotch-potch of styles and period pieces, more reminiscent of a left-luggage office than a presidential palace. The library contained mostly detective novels and the previous President's wife, disliking smoke, had removed all the ash trays. Jackie discovered in the basement a store of beautiful furniture and china stacked away over the years. There was a lot of it but not enough for Jackie's purposes. She had, by this time, decided to do as much as she could for the house historically. She had decided not to redecorate, but to restore.

There was, of course, an immediate outcry. The public were roused by the press to feel this would cause unwarranted expense. In fact it cost them nothing. Jackie aimed for her project to be self supporting. She assembled a committee. The White House had been built in the early nineteenth century, and the plan of the committee set up was to redecorate it to look exactly as it had at the time of its construction, with the help of the incomplete catalogue kept by the National Park Service. It was to be a showplace filled with authentic furniture, period pieces, a place of which the nation could be proud. Jackie's idea quickly became popular and it fitted well with her husband's political ideas for the future of the country. America is great but it could be even greater. For the first few weeks the committee was inundated with offers of furniture from the right period, or such objects as a gilded armchair made for President Monroe (1758–1831) from Miss Catherine Bohlen of Pennsylvania. But there was another way Jackie was going to raise the money needed.

As a child, when they had just moved to Washington from New York, she had been taken round the White House by her mother. At that time there had been no catalogue, and she now decided that catalogues of the house would be eagerly bought by visitors, and that the money from the sale of these could be used for further redecoration. The people who would loan or give the White House pieces were all to be credited. In this way, the repainting necessary to restore the correct colours and any finds that just had to be purchased, were included in the budget. Jackie soon became fascinated by the process, to which she devoted much of her time and energy. When the whole thing was completed, all the people concerned took part in a film to show the transformation that had taken place. The famous newscaster, Charles Collingwood, was taken on a guided tour by the First Lady, who pointed out what had been done, and explained the history of many of the newly acquired pieces of furniture. The film took a whole day to make, and at the end everyone was exhausted—except Mrs Kennedy herself, whose performance, despite the enormous amount of information she had had to learn, was word-perfect—almost too perfect, in fact. The show was as slick as the slickest to come out of the television studios. The information was fascinating. But we all knew as little about the life that went on in the White House as before, while Jacqueline herself remained as much of a mystery as ever. The show was favourably received, but there was disappointment abroad.

Jackie was never to understand the voracious fascination that she and her family were to inspire. The Kennedys, wise to the ways of the press, with whom they would often play a clever game of cat and mouse, were both careful and particular about the kind of publicity they received. Jack was the first President to give impromptu talks to the press and his wife instigated the practice of offering the pressmen drinks beforehand. They were a well loved couple. Beautiful colour pictures would appear of the children with their parents. Suddenly nothing would be heard, nothing would be forthcoming from 1600 Pennsylvania Avenue. Then Jackie, perhaps unwittingly, would suddenly appear, lushly glamorous at some occasion, or casually walking with her children almost in public view in the grounds of the White House. Occasional pictures would whet the public's appetite, but they were never able to satisfy their growing curiosity. The stories that appeared were interesting . . . but never real. The President and his wife were constantly calm, constantly happy, constantly entranced by their children. Those lucky enough to obtain an interview would tend to fall over themselves in admiration of the most obsequious kind. Both the Kennedys were sardonic, wise, slightly arch and they were not to be taken in by the easy flattery of the press. It was hard for them to understand the effect that such articles produced—a mixture of fascination and incredulity, admiration, but also a certain malicious expectancy that something might destroy that rosy dream. So, when nothing came to substantiate such suspicions, a more vicious kind of publicity began.

Since Jackie's absences from her husband's side, the story of their unhappiness was frequently whispered. Close friends and Jackie herself, by her continual care and closeness to him, especially at the first, disproved this. Then a previous marriage was invented for the President. Having plumbed the depths of this imaginary scandal, the press would watch for the children, or report that Jackie was again pregnant. When all else failed they would return to that American obsession, money. One of Jackie's most well-thought-out parties was for Ayub Khan, then President of Pakistan. She felt that Mount Vernon, America's most ancient home and formerly George Washington's farm, would be a more interesting place for dinner than the White House. The guests journeyed romantically up the Potomac river and dinner was served in a pavilion, almost under the stars. The floor of the pavilion was dark green and the table under the yellow ceiling was draped with golden cloths and set with gold china—an inspiring reminder of the wealth of the western world. In keeping with Kennedy custom, the dinner was French and a far cry from the steak and ketchup days of previous Presidents. The menu included Crabmeat Mimosa, and *Couronne de riz Clamart*—hardly sturdy American dishes.

The outcry of 'where does the money come from' was huge. Jackie was hurt and upset, but the furore died down a little when the press actually went to work and discovered that it had not been such an expensive snack after all. After this, entertaining was more or less kept to the White House, but still in the same superb style. Guests were often entertained by such performers as Pablo Casals and orchestras conducted by Leonard Bernstein. As John Steinbeck said, 'Syntax no longer is subversive in the White House.' The popular send-up record of the time mentioned these names and afterwards added the joke, as if coming from the President, 'why always *your* friends, Jackie?' Joking apart, however, it was all her doing. Jack Kennedy liked the company of politicians or his family and at the time of his marriage had been very much a steak-and-chips man. His wife introduced French food into the household, and it was she who invited the artists to their home. Her husband enjoyed such innovations and grew particularly fond of the company of contemporary writers and poets. On one occasion a dinner was given in honour of all American winners of the Nobel Prize. At a time when the typical American in the eyes of the world was an absurd figure clad in Bermuda shorts and a loud shirt, smoking a cigar and displaying a laughable philistinism on all things un-American, the impact of the Kennedy intelligence and love of culture was world-wide. Jackie was the source of this change and the adulation of the American people was reflected in this joke. A young boy, asked what he would like to be when he grows up—a doctor perhaps, an architect or a lawyer—replies promptly, 'No, I want to be a Kennedy!'

Privately the Kennedys were enjoying their roles. The President found his job more rewarding than even he had thought it would be before that snowy day in January. There were difficulties and dramas such as the Bay of Pigs escape, the US support of Cuban exile forces attempting to retake Cuba from Castro, a terrible thirteen days during which the President, his brother and colleagues confronted the Russians and in the end withstood the pressures that were brought to bear by Kruschev. And there were other smaller crises. Jack Kennedy, however, was a man who enjoyed such power and he was an able administrator. During the evenings he was at last able to relax with his wife. 'I spend my days with politicians, not my nights too,' he once said. 'I don't want to come home from the Senate and then have to defend my position to my wife all evening.' Eunice, his closest sister, always said, 'Jack has never made a good job of relaxing, but Jackie has gone a long way to change that.' And in defence of his sister-in-law—who did not, like the others, adore the campaign trail with the cheers, the shouts and the tussle with the crowd—Robert remarked 'at least when he (the President) gets home he knows he won't be greeted with, "How's the situation in Laos today?" ' She was not, in short, the sort of woman she had met and been horrified by—the tough organiser of campaign committees and cheer leaders with the brittle, effusive manner of those other ladies on the periphery of political society. Jackie was certainly not one of those. She did well what it was necessary for a First Lady to do and doubtless enjoyed the adulation. She was, however, easily bored by politics itself and, as she had earlier, she often withdrew into herself. She hid this as well as she could from her husband but, nonetheless, was irritated by the amount of time that he was obliged to spend on his new job. She spent holidays in the white-fronted cottage at Hyannis Port, which she had decorated with simple old New England furniture in cane and wicker work and flowered walls. Here, she would go into one of the spare rooms and paint, not in a relaxed way, but with furious speed, wanting to cover the canvas quickly. She would go for long, lonely walks, leaving the children behind to join in with the rumbustious games of their cousins. Water ski-ing was also one of her favourite pastimes. In the spring and autumn she would hunt with the Orange County Hunt Club of Virginia near their rented house, Glen Ora, or later near their home Atoka which she later named Wexford. Glen Ora was an elegant house, with formal French gardens and both she and her husband preferred this to the President's official retreat Camp David back in the woodlands. Jackie herself was particularly fond of the house with its rooms full of French furniture. A wall in one of the rooms was completely covered with an old map of Paris.

Such days of relaxation were few and she chafed at their rarity. The days in the capital were, even at the most relaxed moments, a strain. It was always necessary to speak cautiously, there were so many people who could, and would, report the most inconsequential conversation to an eager press. Even their evenings were hardly ever their own and were nearly always filled with meetings or official parties. When possible, Jackie would go to Virginia on her own and, as time went by, such occasions became more and more frequent. The family's own quarters at the White House are very small, and she would often feel the need to escape their confines. The dining room was small, and the sitting room not much larger. The Abraham Lincoln room at the end of the corridor was used as a study by the President, and Jackie would often have to walk with a pram past rows of men waiting to see her husband. But there were still the marvellous Christmasses at 601 North County Road in Palm Beach, Florida. The street was lined, as was the whole town, with sub-tropical plants. The sun would shine and the whole family would unite at Joseph Kennedy's house for Christmas lunch and a great opening of presents.

The White House was again full of the antiques Jackie loved so much. The windows were wider than their original Regency counterparts and there were blinds to keep out the sun, but there was a beautiful old spiral staircase. She had always to cover even beautiful marquetry work or parquet floors with carpeting, lest her husband slip and hurt his back again. Jack had been having trouble with his back for several years now. His life had, till then, been constantly interrupted and accompanied by pain and illness. As early as 1935 his studies at the London School of Economics were cut short by jaundice; then, while at Harvard, the major trouble of his life started for which he was twice to be administered the last rites of the Church—his back. He fell on frozen ground while playing football. He was weakened further by malaria in the war. During his second campaign for the Senate, in 1954, he declared he could stand the pain no longer and refused to wear crutches. Despite warnings that he had only a slim chance of recovery, he decided to undergo a lengthy and difficult operation on his back. The surgeons were to try and fuse two of his spinal discs. The operation only partially succeeded. He lay for weeks in a dark room not knowing whether he would live or die. His parents were called more than once to his bedside in the belief that he was dying, but eventually he pulled through. Later on, during his presidency, a specialist, Dr Janet Travell, noticed that his legs were of slightly uneven length. Special shoes corrected the imbalance, and he was, though not cured, much more comfortable. He swam everyday in a heated pool in the White House, but his brother Bobby was to say, later, that half his days on earth had been spent in intense physical pain.

When he returned from the difficult confrontation with Kruschev in Vienna his back gave him a lot of trouble. The days had been strenuous and the travelling took its toll of both of them. They had come to Vienna via Paris and, as the *Boston Sunday Globe* noted, the official run down on Mrs Kennedy's activities alone had shown that she had shaken hands no less than eight thousand and forty-two times, while her hand had been kissed eight hundred and sixty-seven times in all. When Jackie went to see the Lippizanns at the Spanish Riding School —horses trained to perform to music—she must have been relieved that the horses, at least, had no wish to make her acquaintance in this way. The trip to Vienna was wonderful. For Jackie the most moving moment was the Mass in St. Stephen's Cathedral—a magnificent example of Gothic and Renaissance art and architecture. The Vienna Boys Choir sang hymns, the music was by Mozart and the Cathedral was lit by tall candles. For Jackie, moved to tears during the service, it was a great emotional experience.

Their trip to Paris had been a little more worldly. Jackie had, by now, been virtually banned by public outcry from patronising the Paris couturiers, so she selected Oleg Cassini— the brother, oddly enough, of 'Cholly Knickerbocker' Igor Cassini, her first newspaper admirer—who had designed some beautiful clothes for her. But when she wanted to compliment her hosts, she said, she would choose a ball gown from her favourite Givenchy. Her husband never failed to be dazzled.

In Paris, too, the famous hairdresser, Alexandre would come twice a day to tend to her hair, and coil it at *à la* St Catherine by Crivelli—Gothic Madonna style—and once in the style of the Duchess of Fontages, mistress of the Sun King, Louis XIV. Her lipstick, Tender Red, became a sellout hit with the ladies of France! It was here that Jack Kennedy made his famous statement at the Luncheon given for him at the Paris Press Club. 'I am the man who accompanied Jacqueline Kennedy to Paris and I have enjoyed it!'

The years of 1961 and 1962 sped by. On her trips Jackie proved to be the most useful companion an American President could wish for. She stunned those who could not understand her and most particularly she stunned those who could. When she spoke in French or Italian they went wild in the streets. Everywhere, the Jackie look was in. Shop-window models took on the wide face, the snub nose and the brown-eyed look. She was the only woman to disprove the theory that gentlemen prefer blondes. To look like her with that bouffant hairstyle and that flat boyish figure seemed the best thing that could happen to a girl, anywhere. Those years of 1961 and 1962 showed Jack Kennedy the right road for the United States, for himself in power and for Jackie Kennedy.

The separations were still frequent. She travelled to India. The papers were critical of her image there. She often appeared late, they said, or was too busy to allow the waiting crowds to glimpse her. And at one function she left early. But one thing was sure, nothing could stop the young Kennedys going on for another four years. Jackie also travelled to Italy for a holiday with her sister, Princess Radziwill. There, despite the *papperazzi*, she and her daughter managed to enjoy an almost ordinary holiday, although it is not everyone who has the chief of Fiat, Gianni Agnelli, to escort them. She was photographed in a flowered swimsuit, and people wondered if it was reticence that made this glamorous jet-setter fight shy of a bikini, forgetting the marks left by Caesarian birth. Like all women who have had such an operation, Jackie still carries the scars.

When it was announced, in 1963, that she was to have another baby America was as thrilled and glad as if it expected the birth of a Crown Prince. Stories about her present children and future children abounded. It was assumed that this might well be her last child; women who have children by Caesarian section are generally advised to have only three. And Jackie, who would be giving birth to her fourth, had already suffered much for her children. In preparation, Jackie abandoned her riding and the more strenuous duties of the First Lady, and looked forward to the summer she would spend at Hyannis Port, surrounded by her young nephews and nieces.

The year proceeded. The President was confronting difficulties in Congress over his programme of reform—Civil
Rights, Medicare, and so on. Progress was slow, but meanwhile the America for which he hoped was getting closer.
Jacqueline's absence from the White House functions at which
she had previously acted as hostess must have been hard.
Although long separations of this kind were something to
which they had both grown accustomed, yet Jack Kennedy was
worried about the birth of this child. He visited her at Hyannis
Port and, seeing her happiness, was reassured. Affairs of state
were pressing and he was prevented from staying for any length
of time. The baby was not due for five weeks or so. He was
always reluctant to leave—the last time he had set off for
Florida, only to turn the plane in mid-air in order to stay for a
short while longer.

On 7 August, Jackie, knowing that her children missed her
rides with them—particularly John—John who had just
started—took them out in the pony trap. All at once she
realized that the baby was putting in an early appearance.
Keeping as calm as she could she turned the trap round and, on
returning to the house, was rushed to the Otis Air Force Base
Hospital, which had recently acquired a special maternity unit.
Here, again by Caesarean section, she gave birth to a baby boy.
President Kennedy, thrilled by the thought of a second son,
raced to the hospital. They called the child Patrick, after the
first Kennedy to cross the water and Bouvier after Jackie's
family.

Their joy was brief. Like some premature babies the child
had hyaline membrane disease. The President went with the
baby to the Children's Hospital Medical Centre in Boston
where he was placed in a high pressure chamber to help weak
breathing. The President looked at him through the glass, and
then the specialists took over but, in spite of all their efforts
and prayers, Patrick was only to live for thirty-nine hours and
twelve minutes. Jack Kennedy walked into a nearby boiler

room in the hospital, and wept. Ashen-faced he left the hospital to speed back to his wife. Her obstetrician answered her constant questions and had to tell her her son was dead. He prescribed a sedative and somehow she slept until her husband reached her.

Their loss this time was terrible. The family crowded round with love and help, but alone they spent two hours staring at the facts trying to believe the terrible truth. Marriage can be made or broken by such things. After this tragedy husband and wife were cemented together as they had never been before. They promised themselves more children if Jackie's health could stand it, and they vowed to stay together more than heretofore. The separations would not be of their making. Jackie herself was now determined that she would go with him, every and anywhere now, for she had seen that time was moving on. Looking at her husband and her children, she counted her lucky stars.

But before they were reunited it was arranged that she was to convalesce, cruising on the yacht of Aristotle Onassis. The magnificent yacht *Christina* was put at her entire disposal, and Onassis himself, always a considerate host, took care to impose no limits on her wish for solitude.

Bachrach

The Kennedy family sitting in the garden at Hyannis Port in the summer of 1934. From left to right, Joseph Jr. (killed during World War II), Patricia (later Mrs Peter Lawford), Rosemary, Eunice (Mrs Robert Shriver). Seated from left to right, Kathleen (killed in a plane accident in 1948), Robert, Mrs Joseph Kennedy, John, Joseph Kennedy, Edward and Jean (Mrs Stephen Smith).

Ladies Home Journal

12 September 1953, after the wedding of Jacqueline Bouvier
to John Fitzgerald Kennedy. Jackie's sister Lee, to the left of
Jack Kennedy, was Maid of Honour, and Bobby Kennedy
stands on Jackie's left-hand side.

Ladies Home Journal

After the wedding, the new Mr and Mrs John F Kennedy leave for their honeymoon in Acapulco.

Curtis-Atkins

On the day of the Presidential Inauguration in January 1960, the new President and Mrs Kennedy take part in the official procession.

Cornell Capa

Ticker Parade for the Kennedys, 1960.

Camera Press

Mrs Kennedy, on the steps of the White House, greets
Queen Farah and the Shah of Persia, at a Reception on
10 May 1962.

Ladies Home Journal

John Junior, Jackie, Caroline on pony, "Leprechaun", the
late President at the family vacation retreat, Glen Ora, in
Middleburg, Virginia, 1963.

Black Star

Dallas High Street, November 1963. The Presidential cavalcade shortly before the assassination.

Camera Press

Flanked by her two brothers-in-law, Robert and Edward
Kennedy, Jacqueline Kennedy attends the funeral of her
husband, John F Kennedy, on 25 November 1963.

Black Star

On holiday in Italy, with Caroline and Anthony, son of
Jackie's sister, Princess Lee Radziwill.

Camera Press

Jackie Kennedy rides in a fiesta in Seville in 1966.

Harvey

Jacqueline Kennedy listens to a speech by Antonio Garrigues, the man she was reputedly about to marry.

Fred Ward

After the wedding of her half-sister, Janet, in July 1966, Jackie Kennedy talks to Prince Stanislas Radziwill, her brother-in-law, and Arthur Schlesinger. Although she is almost a chain-smoker, this is one of the only existing pictures of Mrs Kennedy smoking a cigarette.

Dennis Brack

The 60,000 ton carrier, *John F Kennedy*, is launched, on
27 May 1967 by Mrs Kennedy and her two children.

Jackie Kennedy leaves the *Christina* with
her children just before her marriage to
Aristotle Onassis.

The new Mrs Aristotle Onassis emerges
from the church on the arm of her husba

Chapter 6

AFFECTIONATELY, LYNDON

So the Kennedys recovered from the death of Patrick. On her return from Greece, Jackie absorbed herself with the other children—Caroline, particularly, had been disappointed by the non-appearance of the eagerly awaited baby—and spent time with her mother and her in-laws, particularly Bobby's wife, Ethel, and her many children. The comforting rough and tumble of family life after the lush cloistering of the *Christina* appealed to her now. Her long, sad reflections offered no real comfort or explanation. In a brave attempt at recovery, she decided to throw all her energy into the activity of her husband's political career.

Her husband needed her at his side. With her chic, trim figure and natural glamour, she was a vote-winner—she was determined not to let a single ballot slip escape the persuasion of her smile. 'Jackie-eee' they would call; she would not disappoint them.

That November she spent some time alone at their weekend house in Atoka, in Virginia. After a long time she rode again, taking Caroline and John-John with her. Again the Kennedys were apart, but not for long. She intimated to her husband that she was willing to enter the electoral fray with him, knowing that he wanted to gain his second term of office and that his hopes for the country's good would only be realised if given enough time. The Congress had blocked much of that which he wished to do and time was short. The months lost waiting for Patrick's birth and those lost recovering from his death, had given time for reflection and time to understand the world of politics from which she had stood aside all this time. During her husband's Presidential campaign she had said that she learnt politics from osmosis, and now, at last, it was becoming something for which she felt enthusiasm. The knowledge of this was like nectar to John F Kennedy.

The Kennedys still had their differences but, bound tighter together by their loss, they determined to go forward as one. The days she spent alone in November were restful for Jackie, and she was able to concentrate her attention on the weeks to come. It would be a success they both vowed. On Wednesday, 20 November, Jackie returned from Atoka to the White House; much earlier than Dr Walsh's expected 1 January she was returning to her post as First Lady. She had said, 'I really do not think of myself as First Lady but of Jack as President.' She was now needed to play more than the role of wife and mother. Politics were to be no longer merely second best and her mind was made up to enter the White House with new determination. That night there was to be a reception for the Judiciary. She would act as hostess of the evening.

She arrived at the White House in the early afternoon and immediately her husband knew she had come she settled down to the usual mass of correspondence. Naturally, the office took care of much of the public correspondence, but Jackie, an inveterate writer since childhood, still had plenty of friends to write to personally. Then there were the children to see. They had left Atoka the day before, and had to get back to their White House lessons.

The list for the evening's party had to be checked and last minute arrangements finalised. It was usually enough to leave everything to the White House staff, efficient, loyal and in their own way party to the Kennedy clan and style; since Jackie had supervised the redecoration of the White House the rooms needed little to prepare them for such an occasion as this. Jackie, who had once said,

I am not much of a cook. I love to read, love to paint, love my house and my baby. I like gardening but I'm not very good at it. I'm better at arranging flowers, would have noted the flowers. The afternoon soon passed, and soon it was time to dress for the evening. A long mulberry dress was laid out in her room.

The First Lady of America leads a lonely life. Often on such evenings the formality of conversation precludes any real feeling of relaxation with assembled guests, and does not encourage the deeper ties of friendship. Like Jacqueline Bouvier Kennedy you had to get dressed, slip into the Yellow Study, a room used to greet visitors, and then telephone for your husband to join the arriving guests.

The reception on 20 November was its usual mixture of White House formality, Kennedy smiles, Washington food and endless handshakes. The judges and their wives, the workers in the Justice departments, had all been carefully invited by the Attorney General. Much of the talk centered around the Kennedys' forthcoming trip to Dallas. The politicians among them realised this was the beginning of the year long campaign, at first to be conducted subtly, but in a few months to develop into a full-scale Presidential Election.

Dallas was a trouble spot in more ways than one. It was in the middle of right wing Texas, one of the states in which Jack Kennedy badly wanted to create the 1964 landslide he had dreamt of since his marginal victory in 1960. Dallas was a large spot of hate in the United States. The United States as two words meant a lot to Jack Kennedy, who insisted that there should be nowhere in these States where the President would not be welcome. Texas is a Southern State and, as such, mostly Democratic in its politics, even though theirs is a distinctly conservative brand. Jack Kennedy's liberal views would make this a hard state to win, even with the help of his Texan Vice-President, Lyndon Johnson, for Texas at that time was one of the few Southern States to have a Republican Senator, John Tower. The feuding within the Democratic party between the right and liberal wings, represented by Governor Connally and Senator Yarborough, was also a grave threat to the success of Jack Kennedy's campaign. His visit to Dallas was particularly necessary at this difficult time and it was to be an attempt both to win the Texan South, while presenting a united front to the country at large. Lyndon Johnson, who was friendly with Connally and yet sympathetic to Yarborough's ideas, was to accompany the party.

Many of the Kennedy team, aware of the political climate in Texas, had advised those closest to him to cancel the visit. Undoubtedly there was widespread hostility. Newspapers branded the President if not as a Communist, at least as a man to be regarded with suspicion. To such men, the supplying of wheat to the Russians, even on a perfectly good sale basis, was almost treason. There were people whose political vision was not merely isolationist, but bordered on xenophobia . . . as applied to non-Texans, not merely to non-Americans.

Only four weeks before, Adlai Stevenson, a father-figure among liberal Democrats and Kennedy's Ambassador to the United Nations, had been screamed at and spat upon by a mob of right-wing 'patriots' in Dallas. Stevenson was gravely disturbed by the ugly atmosphere of hate and reported his fears for the President's safety.

Jackie, however, was determined that the party should be gay. It was Robert Kennedy's birthday, and it was her own first reception in the White House since the death of the baby, Patrick. Such occasions were never particularly relaxed for Jacqueline. Social skill calls for a successful intermingling of guests, and the firm hand of the hostess. So did politicking. Jack would point her in the direction of someone who should have a few words with one of them, while she, too, would keep tabs on people to whom her husband should speak. The President and First Lady could never eat during such receptions, they were too busy. Often they would snatch a mouthful beforehand but in this case they ate afterwards. When their guests had been ushered to a buffet the President left the party to look at some papers, leaving his wife to tend to the guests.

Later, she made her way upstairs to join him for dinner. Patrick's loss had been overcome, physically anyway, she had told her brother-in-law, and she was looking forward to Texas, and a campaign she could join in with. In 1960 she had been pregnant, and something of an unknown entity, her private school ways setting her apart from other politicians' wives. Then her husband's advisers had been secretly rather glad she could not appear at every backwoods stop in her chic French clothes, but now these supposed drawbacks had made her the most popular and slavishly copied First Lady ever, a considerable asset to the Presidential court.

John Connally, anxious that the trip be the best of all possible successes, had asked if Jackie was to accompany the party. The newspapers headlined her agreement and the President remarked on the lesson to be learned, that when you were not around all the time, your attendance was all the more valuable. Black Jack's lesson of elusiveness appeared to be bearing fruit. Jackie prepared to barnstorm the country.

On the evening of Wednesday 20 November, after Robert and Ethel Kennedy had left for a birthday party at Hickory Hill, Jack and Jackie had a quiet meal together. The whole family were home and Caroline and John-John slept a few rooms away. Jackie was glad to feel part of the whole thing again. Jack, eager for her company on the long campaign ahead, was determined that the visit to Texas should run as smoothly as possible. He asked to see her clothes so that they could be sure that the right things would be available at the right time. Sartorial simplicity was something they both liked and, for the rigours of the visit to Texas, the brassy millionaire country where women were even known to wear their minks in the hot noonday sun, it was a necessity.

Jackie was going to wear fine wool in beige and white, blue and yellow, and a pink Chanel suit with navy blouse and matching hat. The weather was going to be cool and there would be some open car riding, for in order to get the maximum effect, one must be seen. Jackie therefore asked for several of her by now famous pillboxes to be packed—they suited her and would not hide her from the crowd, while they would also keep her hair in place in the open car. Although Kenneth, her hairdresser, says, 'She cares less about her appearance than many other women, but puts beauty care automatically into her routine', she was determined to make the visit to Texas a success, and had become accustomed to the constant presence of photographers.

For Jackie, politics were still something of an ordeal and perhaps still something of a bore. Less so than at the beginning but she still found it difficult to accept the momentary intimacy of the political hand-shake, the welcome of strange faces in unfamiliar surroundings. She was, after all, she always felt, only married to the President, not in the seat of power itself. But to America her image was one of immense queenliness and refinement. Jackie was already a legend in the land, unaware of what the next two days would bring.

For Jack Kennedy, the approaching trip was a worry. Those closest to him knew that he, who enjoyed throwing himself into the vote-catching fray, did not approach this campaign, for that it really was, with his usual excited enthusiasm. He was watchful and on edge—a habitual sufferer from covert nervousness, whose hands would tremble as he delivered a speech, despite the calm delivery and the coolness of his manner. Yet he had never seemed so full of trepidation as he seemed before the trip to Dallas that year.

Dallas was no ordinary American city. It had voted less for Kennedy than any other major city in 1960. It was a new raw city built on the new dazzling wealth of East Texan oil. Its inhabitants liked to think of themselves, riding to work, white-collared, in their huge cars, as hard-riding gun-toting guardians of the Old Frontier. The New Frontier was not for them. Dallas was physically violent too, with one of the highest annual murder rates in the USA—about the equal of that for the whole of England. And you could buy a gun in Texas as easily as a plate of beans.

Kennedy, who objected to fanaticism above all things, was angered by the rasping, illogical hatred that poured from the right-wing Dallas newspapers, which accused him of fostering Communism, of treason. A poster put up in Dallas that day read, 'Wanted for Treason', and it referred to the President. They resurrected the hoary old accusation that he had previously been married and divorced. Thus did gun-happy Dallas wear its moral hat when the President came to visit.

The day of Thursday, 21 November started off normally. The Spanish maid, Provi, woke her mistress by gently drawing the curtains. The children were ready to come in. Caroline was already dressed, she had to be at school at nine-fifteen. After a little time with her mother and brother she decided to go down and have breakfast with her father. She knew that he was going to Texas that day. She went downstairs, followed by John, and they breakfasted noisily, with a lot of joking. Soon it was time to leave and the little girl kissed her father and said goodbye. He looked back, waved her out of the door, and she was gone in a twinkling. John, who had not yet started school, was able to stay . . . and he was to see his parents take off in the plane.

Jackie was still dressing for the journey. The night before she had received messages from her family to take care and enjoy the trip. She was soon ready and waited for the rest of the travellers by the Rose Garden. The day was overcast, but her husband had discovered it was to be hot down South. The information, however, had come too late. Jack himself well knew the discomfort of long, hot campaigns fought in heavy clothes, but the cases were packed and it was time to leave. He hoped the weather reports were exaggerated. It was, after all, November.

The helicopter was waiting to take them to Air Force One, the Presidential plane at Andrews Air Base. The White House was so large that the three helicopters had been loaded up before

Jackie noticed. Clint Hill—Secret Service agent—and General Clinton went to collect her. The helicopter carrying her and the President was first off. John-John, who loved flying, sat on his father's knee. The President looked down on Washington which had meant so much to him in these three years. The short trip over, the helicopters descended from the sky, the propellers slowly stopped and the family disembarked. At this stage all the members of the Presidential party who were to accompany the group knew exactly where they would be sitting in the motorcades, and in the three aircraft making their way across the United States to Texas. Each member, for the purposes of easy identification, had been issued with a lapel badge. The same badges were used for every trip the President took, but the colours were changed each time. For the November 1963 trip to Texas the pin colours were blood-red on white.

It was now time for John-John to say goodbye. He hugged his parents and then began to cry. He wanted to go with them. The President had made many trips without his son, but his son was now old enough to appreciate his absence, and it was a sad leave-taking. To avoid the glare of publicity, from which Jackie had tried to shield her children since the Inauguration, the Kennedys decided to leave John Jr. in the helicopter. Sadly leaving their son, in the care of his Secret Service agent on what was known as the kiddie-detail, the President and his wife left the helicopter and mounted the steps into Air Force One.

The plane, made especially for the President, his seal covering everything from the ashtrays to the carpet, was both work place and rest place for Jack and Jacqueline Kennedy. Jackie preferred the privacy of the front to the activity of the main cabin. She was not interested in taking part in the political discussion, but would rather read or in this case work with her secretary Pamela Turnure on the Spanish speech she was to make next day to the League of United Latin-American Citizens.

At length they arrived at San Antonio to be greeted by the Vice-President and Mrs Johnson, who in Texas were on their home ground. But the crowd was for Mrs Kennedy who appeared out of the Presidential plane with 'The United States of America' flashed down its fuselage, in a white dress with a black leather belt and black beret, smiling her rather shy smile. The call went up . . . 'Jackieeee, Jackieeee'.

The day was a rough one. Yellow roses were pressed into the First Lady's hands. The people wanted not just to see her but to touch, almost to taste, the glamorous object of their fascination. Jackie herself had eyes mainly for the children, who seemed both more understandable and more humane, and whose awed excitement held less violence. Each day, at school, they made their Pledge to the Nation. It mentioned the President and here he was, and she was just a lady holding flowers. The thought was simpler.

The cars soon stood before her. Cool and poised amid the *mêlée*, Jackie, who seemed to know instinctively where to go, always lent an air of gentility and slow purpose to the flurry of such occasions. Jack, too, was an imposing figure—the Kennedy sense of style showed wherever they walked. The day was a hubbub of speeches, drives and people, and they were glad to reach Houston later that day. Jackie had been frightened by the agitation of the crowd, women sobbing for her to touch them, and when she had approached them they had hardly let her escape. The quiet moments alone with her husband in the bedroom of the Presidential plane had been restful, but when they had re-emerged from the welcome captivity of the plane, the crowds again separated them. In the car they could rarely speak, obliged to turn to their own sides, wave, and widely smile. As Dave Powers said when asked to assess the crowd by the President, 'For you, about the same as last time you were here, but a hundred thousand have come to look at Jackie.'

The hotel at Fort Worth was a welcome stop. The room Jackie had been assigned was quiet but ugly, with nothing but drab green walls, and a window that overlooked the neon-lit parking area. Jackie spoke to her husband before going to bed, and they arranged for her to be at breakfast at nine-fifteen—he was to make a speech before then, but she had no need to be there. The going for the future campaign, if it was to be anything like today, was to be tough. The number of the Kennedy suite was 850, the numbers of which added together came to one always associated with superstition . . . and often bad luck . . . thirteen!

The next day Jackie, who had laid her clothes out the night before (Mary Gallagher, her maid for the trip, had somehow got lost), slowly got dressed. She had chosen the pink Chanel-style suit which was a favourite of hers, and in which she felt particularly comfortable. She tied the bow of the silk blouse into a knot and tucked it into the jacket. A large bow would only flap around and look untidy in photographs. It took her some time to complete her toilet and the President, below in the car park lot, was asked where his wife was. 'Mrs. Kennedy is organizing herself', he replied, smiling, 'It takes her a little longer but, of course, she looks better than we do when she does it.'

Jackie was ready to descend, but she had no idea that she was to enter a ceremonial breakfast. She had just remarked to Mary Gallagher that a day on the campaign road could age a person thirty years, though of course no-one else could see it in *her* face, when she was ushered into breakfast almost with guns firing a salute and drums rolling. Rather taken aback and unaccustomed to being alone at such a gathering, she looked for her husband . . . and finding him with her eyes walked towards him. Her hands, in short white gloves, made the familiar nervous gesture of pushing her hair away, as much a shield against hair as they were against people, noise, crush, but soon she reached the top table. A smile from the President and they were seated. The presents from the Texans were given and gratefully received. There were speeches. A whole event was made out of breakfast, in a way that was, for America, quite usual. The breakfast party is a New World invention. For the First Lady it was a plunge into the old world of before November 1960.

The walls that had seemed so drab the night before were hung with beautiful paintings, loaned from the collections of Liberal Democrat well-wishers. Jackie and Jack were touched.

Jackie had made a big hit, and at the end of it all, Al Otten of the *Wall Street Journal* asked Dave Powers if Jackie was going to feature heavily in the future electoral campaign. He realised her publicity worth and satirically asked if she was going to come out of a cake next time. Dave Powers drew himself up into his sardonic best and retorted fast, 'She's not that kind of bunny'. In the next hour or so the lady in question had in fact decided that though she would not be emerging as confectionery, she would be emerging. Her husband, delighted to hear she would come with him campaigning, asked her if she could make California in a fortnight's time. Their lives had been pulled apart for so much of their marriage that neither of them simply expected the other to be at such and such occasion as a matter of course. They would book up each others diaries as if dear old friends. The First Lady averred she would be delighted.

They were soon out on the open road again to the Presidential plane, onward to the capital of this State, Dallas, the town they called Big D. They had thirteen flying minutes, thirteen again, to go. Mrs Kennedy, like many women fairly superstitious, took no notice. The family flew so often, that a short flight of this kind was routine. Everything seemed to be going well, despite the black rumours about Texas, and she could not imagine anyone throwing so much as a tomato at the President. The crowds seemed enraptured.

They again descended the ramp to the ground, the band playing the special presidential song, *Hail to the Chief*—her husband's favourite song, she had once jokingly remarked,

They were in Dallas at an airport named Love Field. The crowd was welcoming, cheering, but there were some anti-Kennedy placards too. Jackie was too busy to notice them at first, waving with one hand and holding a large bunch of red roses in the other. The red went none too well with the pink of her suit, and she wondered why this Texas town had varied from the others and offered her not yellow roses but deep red ones.

The motorcade of the most powerful man in the world moved slowly off. It was sunny and hot. Jackie concentrated on the crowd, her gaze irresistibly drawn to the anti-Kennedy placards, but happily she could not read many of them. On the outskirts of the town the reception was not enthusiastic, they waved, but the crowd was a little reserved, almost hostile. Jackie, never over-fond of the loud, rumbustious crowds, suddenly missed them. Evidently there were not many votes in this one, and sometimes the kerb sides were completely empty. The sun was blazing, and when there was no-one there to see she put on her large sunglasses, but the minute they entered the city centre, and the crowds increased, she removed them at the President's request. The Kennedys and the Connallys had to acknowledge this turn-out. Both of the couples, in different ways, with relief. They came to some children, the car stopped and the President reached out for their open hands. By Live Oak Street the crowds were really wild with delight. Kennedy was smiling. Jackie's white-gloved hand waved in response to their calls. They went down Main Street. The sun was hot. The signs read 'All the Way with JFK'. The car travelled slowly down Main Street, snaking its way along towards the Trade Mart, the next stop. The large shiny limousine with its cargo of five, the centre of the action, seemed to enjoy slowing down, giving them all a chance to see the President, and his wife. They both waved at the world, the world waved back. Except for one man.

They entered Elm Street. Jackie could see a tunnel ahead and looked forward to the cool of its shadow. It was a shadow that spread across the Texan day. Thinking she heard motor cycles backfiring, she continued her smiles. Suddenly she heard a scream, and looking to the front saw and heard a terrified John Connally shout 'No, no, no, they're going to kill us all.' Wondering why he should be shouting like that, the First Lady finally looked round at her husband, leaning forward to understand his face, his beloved face. Questioning. He raised his hand to his head, but in a shattering second it fell back. A bullet had spliced the President's skull.

At that moment it was the centre of the world inside the back of the large, shiny car—a man's face, but his head blown open, and a crooning, bending, loving woman who has shouted to the crowd, to God and herself, 'My God, what are they doing? My God, they've killed Jack, they've killed my husband, Jack, Jack.' But he will never answer her. Jackie unwary for herself, forces herself over the back of the car, which is now moving off and out of the horror area perilously fast, to help Clint Hill, the fastest man in Dallas that day. For seconds both of them, one clambering ungainly in high heels and a skirt, the other, arm flaying, trying to pull himself to his President, are in danger too. Clint Hill climbs into the car, and Jackie bends down and holds the President in her arms. He is, she feels sure, dead. Over and over, in a strangled voice, she calls that she loves him, that she loves him. Only the woman in the front, holding her own badly wounded husband, hears her. Clint Hill, full of tears and anger and frustration hears too. Looking down on the red scene, he watches the First Lady pull down the red roses. They hid the larger red area, but they were not enough. Her hands and arms shaded the President as they had never done before, she wanted no-one to see. Her hat slipped and she tore it off with vehemence, full of sickening anger and terror. She was trying to cover the uncoverable, heal the unhealable . . . the car was filled with blood torn from his brain. The world and the siren of the car were whining, long and plaintively.

Jacqueline Kennedy was unaware of the many movements of the motorcade. The car at last drew up at the hospital, but they could not dislodge her husband from her arms. A Secret Service agent, trying to find out which President he should be protecting, tried to see if President John F Kennedy was still alive. He peremptorily asked her to get up. She did not, could not, would not move. He lifted her elbow, and looked at the face—impossible to know the heart was still beating. He immediately walked over to Lyndon Baines Johnson.

Jackie was not left in privacy. Her husband's beloved friends and Secret Service agents surrounded the car silently in horror. She tried to hide him further, and bowed low her head. His face touched her breast. She choked out cries no-one but those closest could hear. Eventually she stopped, and raised her head, her face was wooden, hard, and no tears were visible.

Again they, who loved him too, asked for his body to be taken into the hospital. Jackie remembers she moaned and said she was not going to let him go, pleadingly saying 'You know he's dead. Let me alone.' Suddenly Clint Hill, knowing intuitively what she was trying to do, wordlessly removed his coat and gave it to her. He had seen the head before she had cradled it to her. Together they placed the coat on her lap, and then very, very gently she wrapped the President's head in it. They brought the stretcher forward. Almost with relief she gave up her precious load. But only for an instant . . . the coat was falling away from that head which must not be seen less perfect than it had been a mere twenty minutes before. White-faced and stiff-knuckled, she crouched low over the stretcher, and they entered the hospital. The stretcher was wheeled into the doctors. She fell back and began the wait. The world, who had learned in disbelief of the President's shot wounds, at the time not considered as necessarily serious, tuned in their transistors and listened.

Jackie stood in the hospital corridors and prayed. The

hospital smelled of rubber and ether. She waited and prayed, her face as deathly as her husband's, her legs awash with the thick blood of his veins, her suit strewn with the first hot spurts of his wound. But no tears came. She stood, regal and still, almost, as a wax-work.

Next door John Connally was being attended to. Jackie, sure her husband was dead, asked Nellie Connally for news of her husband. Mrs Connally, still shocked and unhinged by that terrible moment of tragedy in the Dallas streets, looked at her without recognition. She snapped that her husband would be all right. There was to be no comfort. At last someone brought a folding chair, and Jackie Kennedy, heroine of the Texas crowd, slowly sat down.

Nellie Connally drew away. Stunned, the First Lady sat in the chair, amid the feverish activity, and thought to herself, for the first time since it happened, 'Maybe he's alive.' Jacqueline Kennedy had been kept out of too many of her husband's sick-rooms. She rose, and ignoring the nurse who had already tried to pull the bloodstained gloves off her hands, tried to enter. The doctors and nurses, determined to keep the area of operations as clear as possible, responded in the usual way. A nurse, larger and heftier than Mrs Kennedy, barred the entrance. But the slim image of Jacqueline was no indication of her real strength, and of the decision she had just made. She had thought to herself that if only he would live, there was nothing she would not give. She heard he was still alive and she was desperate to be with him. The doctor, George Burkley, who travelled on these trips with the President, overruled the nurse and prevented the impending scuffle. He guided Jackie to his place in the corner. She knelt and prayed for a long time. When she stood up her legs were even further covered with the President's blood. Much of it was on the floor. Determined to stay with her husband until his last second on earth, she was afraid those seconds would pass without a priest and asked for one to be sent.

It was almost one o'clock, and the doctors knew it was too late. Dr Clarke, the man in charge, looked at Jackie, pronouncing with difficulty the words about the fatal shot, but it was George Burkley who, supporting this calm ashen-faced woman, knew that he must tell her clearly, so that she knew without a shadow of doubt. He made out the softest words in his mind, but they came out in the most formal way possible. 'The President is dead.' His tears broke the silence. She leaned her cheek against his, and her face remained almost still.

Some of the doctors moved away to treat other cases. Jacqueline Bouvier Kennedy, now a widow, took her husband's hand, clasped it, gazing at his face. At last a priest arrived to give the President the Last Rites of the Church. Then Jacqueline Lee Bouvier Kennedy left John Fitzgerald Francis Kennedy, went to sit and resume a vigil, a communion, on her small folding chair in the corridor. She thanked the priest in a small whisper, and asked him to pray for the President. Then she leant forward in giddiness. They quickly brought a cool band for her forehead; she had been on the point of fainting.

Her eyes great wells of unhappiness and her body rigid, she stood again. The new First Lady approached; her footsteps, and those of the Secret Service agent guarding her, made a lot of noise. She leaned towards her predecessor, looking slightly up at her. The two brunette heads merged for a moment as Lady Bird Johnson embraced her, spoke some words of sorrow, of consolation. They had never been close but both of them understood the roles that they had to play. When she left, Jackie continued her vigil.

In the calm city of Washington the news broke and spread across the world. The two young Kennedy children still did not know. Their loving guardians, their nurse, Maud Shaw, and their grandmothers, aunts and uncles did not know what to do, nor how to tell them. Their mother was far away, and it was hard to conceive of Jackie, always the bright gay one, the woman with the reputation of being aloof, in the widow's role. She still sat outside her husband's room. The chauffeur of the car, Bill Greer, came and cried on her shoulder. She thanked him for his condolences, again in a quiet whisper. Others came, and wept before her frail stillness, but eventually she could take no more of people's sympathy, and her guard kept watch over her stiff silence. Once or twice again she lurched, giddily, but she never passed out of that awareness that had hit so hard about fifteen minutes after the President had been shot. It was an awareness that was not to leave her in sleep or waking for many days and months.

After difficulties with those who wanted to protect her, she entered the room. The solitary figure was slow to walk to the prone figure of her husband. Away in another world, on the other side of the room, was the undertaker. Jacqueline took her hand from her side and, with O'Donnell's help, unpeeled the bloodstained glove sticking to her hand. She touched the plain ring on the third finger of the left hand, the ring she had worn for ten years, two months and ten days. She had been given it in a Newport church wearing a long, white immaculate dress. Now she was to put it with her husband, the man who had given it to her so many married hours ago. Eventually the ring fitted on his finger. Jackie looked down at it and at her dead husband, longing for privacy, but she knew she would never be left alone with a dead body. She retraced her steps back to her post, and started smoking feverishly, soon finishing her own, and obliged to borrow some . . . a strange priest came to her . . . the local authorities demanded an autopsy. The President's coffin, between the men who loved him too dearly to do their duty to the new President, finally left the hospital. She was still with him, and her gloved hand rested on his casket.

They drove to Love Field. Jackie Kennedy—with two roses from her bouquet that had lain near his heart, saved from the major medicine room by Dr Burkley—watched as her husband, the President, the late President, went aboard first. She followed after and sat as close to it as possible—but on returning to the bedroom that she had left not so many hours before, she saw, horrified, Lyndon Johnson reclining on the bed, his secretary taking notes. Jacqueline Kennedy might, but for this, never have returned to Washington, her body still covered in her husband's blood. Perhaps she would have not been so proud, so silently reproachful had she not seen, in a room she still thought of as her own, which was still full of her things—and his—the sickening evidence of a new world in which she had no place and no importance.

She returned to her seat by the coffin.

They awaited take-off. She wanted to get back to Washington, to the children. After the first crank of the engines, however, the plane became silent, and stood still. It was very hot and the ex-First Lady for the first time became impatient. She wished to leave. But there was another First Lady and President on board, and they had some unfinished business in Texas, their home state. The world saw the pictures the next day. A Jackie Kennedy for once not erect but a little crouched. The President with his right hand raised. So unlike the snowy day of the inauguration, three years before, President Lyndon Baines Johnson took the sacred oath of office. They could finally move out of Texas.

The Kennedy group gazed at the number of Texans and the Johnsons in the stateroom of what was still to them Jack Kennedy's plane, realising that not only had they lost him, but the country had lost him too. As Norman Mailer wrote, 'For a while the country was ours. Now it was their's again.' Jacqueline Kennedy, beside the coffin, for the first time cried. She must have cried her soul dry. The world was not to see another tear. The long, long journey continued, over a United States stunned and mute, waiting and watching.

Jackie, still in her pink suit, stained with blood, was advised to have a drink. She drank the Scotch they gave her, hating the taste. She was never a Scotch drinker, and was afraid it would make her weepy. She did not realise that for the moment her tears were all done. One look at her emergence from the dark side of the plane, holding her brother-in-law's hand and the world wept. She had wanted them to see. In those first moments on the plane, when she had had a choice, she had wanted them to see and know what the world had done.

She told Robert Kennedy of the death of his brother, the story spilling out. He listened, silently, and comforted her as best he could and leant against the coffin too. Unaware of the silent crowds, they drove straight to the Bethseda Naval Hospital. The American way of death was a tasteless one to Jackie; his old service, the Navy, was to handle the details. They entered the large autopsy room. Jackie went first to Ben Bradlee, an old friend, and then to his wife Toni. Her mother, Janet Auchincloss, was there. Mother and daughter wanly smiled and embraced one another.

The Kennedy children had had a strange day of travelling; a short ride that was to take Caroline to friends to stay, to their grandmother's house, then back to their own bedrooms in the White House. The guards surrounding them had been deciding what their actions were. Those poor children, they all thought to themselves. Their grandmother, countermanding her daughter's wish that she would tell Caroline next morning, telephoned Miss Shaw to tell her granddaughter the news. It was to be the hardest moment in the nanny's life, and the longest night. She kept a constant vigil on the little girl's room for the slightest sound.

Meanwhile, at the Bethseda Naval Hospital, there was one recurrent sound—the small voice of the widow, telling the story of Jack's death, telling the story of Patrick's death, purging herself of the horror. They all listened. Eventually it was time to go back to the White House. And after a night of to-ing and fro-ing she eventually went to bed to sleep in the double bed, one side of which was hard board and horse-hair, and there Dr Burkley gave her yet a second sedative. At last, the long day over, she lost consciousness.

After that day the movements of Jacqueline Kennedy and her family were very very public. John had not grasped the enormity of death, nor had the nearly six-year-old Caroline, until taken by her mother to the East Room where, beneath the drapery of the national flag, her father's coffin lay. She held close to her mother, at last shrouded in black, and the movements of their heads to kiss the coffin beneath the flag were shown on television screens the world over. The next day Jackie, heavily veiled, the two children at either side in pale blue coats, and the President's brothers lead the procession, walking slowly after the coffin to the graveside, watched by a sad and silent country. When his widow finally received the folded flag which had covered the President's body, her face, up until this moment so publicly calm, was seen in agony. They were at this moment filling in the grave with cold dark soil. It was all over.

Jackie, at thirty-three years old the embodiment of calmness and majesty, finally let go the mask, the lashed strain of her sorrow. The private woman was behind the veil, and underneath the black gauze, she realised now that she was really alone. Her mother, there with her that day, was proud of her grace, her unfailing knowledge of the right thing to do, and her father too, had he lived to this moment, would have been proud of her aloofness, her majesty, her terrible beauty. The horse who walked in front of the gun carriage was named, like him, Black Jack. The socialising, the expensive tastes, her aloofness, her separations from what was often previously thought to be her duty, were forgotten. In those days when she surrendered to Lady Bird Johnson the role of First Lady, she proved she had always been worthy of it.

Her public role officially finished, the strengths of kindness and real refinement she had always had did not desert Jacqueline Kennedy.

The Sunday after the funeral, she received a letter from her husband's successor. He thanked her admiringly for the strength and thoughtfulness she had shown in ringing him on the Thanksgiving evening. He said that her behaviour had gained for her a place in history. He and Lady Bird would in their turn need her help. He sent her their deep love and signed it 'Affectionately, Lyndon.'

Chapter 7

THE VERY FIRST LADY

THE affectionate letter could do nothing to make the move easier. Power belonged to the inhabitants of the White House and the move had to be a fast one . . . America, stunned by the tragedy of the last days, mourned with the lonely survivors of the Dallas murder. But the new administration and those who looked coldly at the transference of power, knew that the sooner the new President went into his home, the sooner the people of America would recover; they would argue to themselves that the cause lay not with their gun laws, nor the violence of a sick society, the lack of social responsibility and would become convinced that the guilt lay outside the system, and that the tragedy had been a fluke, a quirk of fate. There were always cranks . . . what had it to do with them?

Johnson himself, though distressed and sad, wanted the change. A man of habitual energy and confidence, restraint was not one of his outstanding traits, and besides, the country needed a firm hand to guide it through this dark hour. The episode reflected very badly on Texas, the state he had represented at the Senate, his home state, and he himself must have felt an agonising sense of guilt.

Jackie herself wanted to leave, to rescue her children from the house where every entrance and exit was marked by the flashing of lights and the shouts of newspapermen in strange contrast to the silence of the crowd, who simply waited and stared. She wanted to take them away from the house where they would run down to their father's office and play amid his desk and State secrets.

She wanted to be alone, and at last, after the black veil had been lifted from her face, she wept the tears of a bereft woman, tears that echoed those almost guilty feelings she had had in a corridor at Parkland Hospital, when she felt she would have done anything had he lived. He had died, and she felt sorry for those things she might have done better when he had lived. Could she have stifled her dislike of politics, could she have helped more? She had been slightly aloof from family parties when she refused to join in political dinners in Hyannis Port every night, and Jack Kennedy had wondered, at times. Her love of her own life that sometimes kept his waiting, like the time only this year when she had not hastened back to Washington from the waters of Greece and the Onassis yacht *Christina* as soon as an outcry was raised in the capital about her host—Jack had always indulged her absences. She had attended neither the convention that had elected him Presidential candidate, nor the long night wait when he had finally made the Presidency his. He, of course, worried for her health, had said she should stay at home, but had she insisted, perhaps she could have helped him. And those awful moments in the car. Had she only heard something earlier, had she only shielded him from that second terrible shot. The nights were filled with her recriminations and she could sleep only under heavy sedation.

She would dream of those early years, the years when they holidayed in the South of France and spent much of their time in New York, the years in the little Georgetown house with the baby girl. The week-ends at Atoka where she had gone hunting and riding and taught her children to delight her husband. The year when they fell in love, and she would toil through those hot summer nights translating his political tracts while he would admire the collection of books she brought back from Europe. She would remember the pet names—he was Bunny, she was sometimes Jacks, as she had been to her sister; and Buttons, as her father called Caroline, and John-John, bereft of their father earlier and more completely than she herself had been as a child.

The Averill Harrimans who lived on N Street, the street of her first real married home, were to loan her their house for the first move from the White House. The move, however, had first to be completed. Once decided, Jackie asked help of all those who were not already involved in the movements of the new President, and soon the rooms were stripped. Much, of course, was left. Her hard work at re-decorating the White House with as many original pieces as could be found, had left its mark, and there were her touches everywhere. The books, the French prints and paintings; the porcelain ornaments and beautiful glass vases; beautiful linen, embroidered with initials, and the napkins that matched table clothes and china sets for their personal use. There were also the children's things, toys, books and clothes to be packed. Jack's office had been the first to be cleared out, and the oval room now had a new owner. A few days after the funeral, a leather-backed rocking chair stood on the lawn. Around it was the empty garden, and further back the Rose Garden created to give the President a beautiful view from his office by a family friend, Bunny, Mrs Paul Mellon. There were vast removal vans at this entrance. People hustled and bustled around, waiting for Jackie and the children to leave. They noticed the chair, suddenly, and the crowd quietened. Photographers took pictures of it and most people swallowed, hard. The chair was lifted and loaded into the back, and the van drove away. Then the car moved off, with its precious load. The guard, as usual, saluted. None of them in the car looked back.

The Georgetown house, like Jackie's first one, stood just a few feet from the pavement, and people could, if they wished, stand right by the door. In this house the three of them lived. Caroline and John had aged since their father's death to six and three years; their birthdays had been on the day of his funeral and two days after that.

Friends came to visit, and people sent letters, in their thousands . . . and hundreds of thousands. Her secretary and

long-time friend Nancy Tuckerman helped her answer them.
They were far away from the days of the year-book inscriptions
at Miss Porter's: 'Where to find Jackie, laughing with Tucky.'
Neither of them laughed much now, but got on with
the job. Jackie devoted as much time as she could to her
children. Often she got very annoyed for no reason. Like a
shell-shocked soldier she was now angry, angry with guilt,
regret and sorrow, only wishing those moments in Dallas had
been able to repeat themselves. She would rather have died
instead of him.

At this time her friends, and those who had known her
husband, came forward with a suggestion for a memorial to
the late President, a tribute to his great promise and achieve-
ment. Their suggestion was the foundation of the Kennedy
Library. It was to be set up at Jack Kennedy's old college,
Harvard, and would be financed by donations. It was to be a
centre for Kennedy memorabilia—his letters, the archives
recording his work, the chair in which he sat to rock away the
world's problems. Jackie responded eagerly and gratefully. At
last there was something she could do to help. Her close
friends at this time, as in the years before, were the Ormsby
Gores. They had helped by transferring the school, which
Caroline had attended on the solarium of the White House, to
the British Embassy. Here the few children would continue
their studies until school started again, when Caroline would
be enrolled in an ordinary school. David Ormsby Gore and
his wife had always been close to the Kennedys, and they now
helped, in their quiet English way, to take the load off the
widow. Aiding her in this, at least she knew her daughter
would still be with the same school friends as before. There
were many friends. Robert and Ethel Kennedy saw her often
and at all times took Caroline and John into their family.
Robert became the principal man in her life, and even more
important, he was the same for John who, already at three
years old a typical Kennedy, with much of the Irish chat, and

full of energy, needed a man around to keep him in line. His cousins were training John to be a Kennedy touch-football expert. The first time Robert used his influence was actually at the funeral. Jackie had decreed the children should wear matching blue coats, and white gloves; Caroline wore a black headband round her head as the only sign of mourning. John-John, already a tough, rumbustious little boy, had no truck with gloves. In the car, his mother had asked him to put them on. His uncle Robert had said he did not need them. Again, his mother asked him to put them on. By this time he knew that his uncle was a staunch masculine supporter. The sight of John saluting his father, as the coffin passed in front of him for the last time, was one of the most poignant of the day.

Jackie herself tried to adjust. She cut her hair short and wore it flatter, with a fringe and curled under at the sides. She ordered a fairly extensive widow's wardrobe. The black clothes did not suit her, but she was impervious to this and did not shed her weeds until the Democratic Presidential Convention in the summer of 1964. She went out only when it involved her late husband, and attending a performance of Bach's *Saint Matthew Passion* in Boston she wept openly. She visited Harvard to look at the site of the Kennedy Library. She helped the children with schoolwork, and taught John to read and write with the help of Maud Shaw's additional lessons.

The year could not go by without the usual Christmas trip to Palm Beach. Jackie very much wanted to sit at home and do nothing but, for the children's sake and so that continuity would be sacrificed as little as possible, they went to join the rest of the Kennedy clan. The little Kennedys busied themselves making Christmas presents. Their mother and father had always encouraged them to make things, rather than buy presents for birthdays and Christmas. Jackie had to buy presents for them and the rest of the family, and try somehow to face the seasonal festivities. The number of Christmas wishes and gifts they received was enormous. The Steve Smiths, Robert Kennedys, Peter Lawfords, Teddy Kennedys, Sargent Shrivers, were all there. Joseph Kennedy, dealt another terrible blow by the death of a second son, was host as usual, a role that cost the partially paralysed man much anguish. But the children were to enjoy this time, and riding sessions were arranged with the older children, in which Caroline could take part, while there were games for the younger ones, in which John was a loud and jovial participant. For the widow it brought memories of Christmases past. On their return to Washington, she made yet another of her frequent pilgrimages to the Arlington hillside where her husband lay and prayed alone in the large cathedral in Washington.

The house was a pressing problem. The Harrimans would want to return before long although their boundless generosity left the door of hospitality wide open. And so Mrs Jacqueline Kennedy, widow, sorted out her own affairs and bought a house for herself in N Street again, just a few doors away from the house they had owned whilst Jack Kennedy was Senator. The house was completely empty, and had been so for some time. Jackie again took up something she loved, interior decoration. The house had to be habitable. She surrounded herself with fabrics, furniture, wallpaper, antiques, everything she needed to decorate beautifully a new and larger house. The house again was on three floors, but it was more spacious than both the previous houses on N Street. The children, trailed by their spaniel Shannon, took countless rides in the lift until the novelty wore off. They were lodged on the third floor, and each had a room, again done up in classic blue for a boy and pink for a girl. This time, Caroline was old enough to take note of her new room and her mother promised her that soon she could select a wallpaper for the pink painted walls. On the floor beneath there was a study; Mrs Kennedy's bedroom, dressing room and bathroom and the spare bedrooms; and below this, the dining and reception rooms, kitchen and pantry.

Again Jackie selected the pastel colours that went so well with the antique furniture she and her husband had collected in the early days of their marriage. She interested herself in antique salerooms and bibelot bargains again. But one great necessity for this house was white lace curtains. The house, being so near the pavement, was part of the tourist track. The Jackie watchers, as they were called, would come from all over the world, at all hours of the day. Neither Jackie nor the children could ever leave, the constant watchful eye again intruded on their private life. She was no longer First Lady, and she felt these people to be like stiff marionettes, animated only when she opened and closed the front door. Down in the basement the three Secret Service men would discuss their jobs and the difficulties that these constant crowds occasioned. They could hardly go amid the crowd checking for guns, or explosive. Anything could have happened, but luckily nothing did.

The crowds grated on the Kennedys' nerves. Every movement they made was watched. Jackie knew the people meant well, and were only full of sympathy, but she hated the continual exposure to their inquisitive gaze. Soon, every outfit in her widow wardrobe, every hat, every new hairdo, was photographed and analysed. She began to feel like a wicked woman whose gradual return to life after the death of her husband was something to be ashamed of. She was slowly withdrawing from the Washington world, for which she had no need or preference without the company of her husband. The American capital is a politicians' town, and nothing else really happens there. It is a town with wide, planned boulevards, littered with huge neo-classical public monuments and government buildings. Jackie, at that moment less interested in politics than ever before, decided to move to New York. The Jackie watchers were simply the last straw. The things Jackie loved were in that city, and although it meant leaving the town where her mother and step-father and Robert Kennedy lived, she was determined to go. She made up her mind and, typically, acted fast. She found an apartment in New York at 1040 Fifth Avenue, a ten roomed duplex flat in the smartest part of town. They were moving again.

She left number 3017 N Street Washington for the melting pot of Manhattan, New York. There she joined the world of glamorous society.

New York, though the largest city in the most egalitarian country in the world, has its own rules and its own aristocracy. You count if you have money. But there is a second crowd of that species, where you count if you have money and you spend it in the 'right' way. The 'right' way, if you want to join this group, is easily recognised, and though it might take time, you need the right accent. If you do not have the right background, something creative will do, and you can eventually jump into their well-feathered echelons. You rise quite late and attend, with the help of a social secretary, to correspondence. Thereafter the telephone is employed, to sort out details on your latest clothes, furniture, house and such like. Stocks and shares and money are all taboo at this stage of the morning. If married, your poor hardworking husband has gone to the office hours before, being very careful not to wake you, poor thing, who had such a late night last night. The almost twice-a-week visit to the hairdresser is then required, and possibly you have a manicurist or masseuse at your home.

This is, of course, not unlike the lives of rich women anywhere, but never does it follow such a rigid pattern as it does here. Before you go out you have made arrangements for lunch. These can only be at one of about five restaurants. They are well known, very expensive, snob and chic. If you are lucky, a photographer from *Women's Wear Daily*, the Fairchild paper designed originally for the Seventh Avenue garment trade, will catch you in your latest couture outfit. In you go, to lunch with like ladies. Whereupon you can launch into any topic so long as it is serious. The topics, of course, will be where did you go last night and what happened, and where will you go tonight and what will happen, where did you get that coat and where will you get your next one . . . unless the couturier's handwriting is so recognisable that you simply drop the name and a compliment and discuss his latest collection, and your latest buy (or preferably buys, at many hundred dollars a time) from him. Any other gossip is welcomed, and small variations and rhapsodies upon the same tune of your mutual success in life with husbands, lovers, children, children-in-law, Art (capital A), and social work are allowed, in small doses. Thereafter, and after a small, low calorie lunch, at which you have fiddled with your food (Bunny Mellon is known for her quote, 'No girl can be too rich or too thin'), food which has cost a small fortune, you go off to achieve success with the above.

Return to your luxurious home, which can only be on certain streets between certain numbers, possibly for a small nap. Bath and change before your husband comes home and greet him with a cocktail in your hand—his cocktail, you don't drink much, yet. Thereafter a dinner party, or a charity ball at one of the good hotels; possibly the theatre, if it is a fashionable play, or the ballet or the opera, then home, fairly drink-filled, to a late night. The breaks in this 'dreadful' round consist of holidays, short good-weather trips around America, both North and South, but basically the whole thing is a keep-up job, whether its with the latest table linen, or handbag.

Just in case you are not recognised as belonging to the 'Beautiful People'—for this is the name of the Girl Guide pack, which also includes some beautiful boys—you have a uniform. Your face, beautifully taken care of at one of the top cosmetic salons, is well, if a little over, made-up. Try never to appear without your false eye-lashes. Your hair, which is naturally full (probably streaked, with blonde strands, as if you have just returned from a sun-drenched holiday, whatever the time of year) is long, and wide and sometimes slightly wild. It will be supplemented by a full, long, false piece of hair expertly matching your own, so that only you, your hairdresser and all the other women like you wearing one, will know. You will wear expensive clip earrings during the day, possibly drop ones at night. The simple gaberdine dress you wear will be worth a dollar a stitch, and in the winter you will cover it with a sumptuous mink, which each year has its own smart accessory—a jewelled belt, or double breasted style . . . you may be sure it is never the same mink. Name (only the top three designers) bags and shoes will be worn; add the short white leather gloves which Jackie actually made famous and dark silk sheer tights and, if a little tired, big big shades (sunglasses). No one can fail to notice you. There are copyists, of course, but if you watch carefully you will always be that one distinctive step ahead of the rest. It is a full-time, fun-time job.

It was a crowd that had distinct fascination for Jackie. At first she was not interested, the work on the Kennedy Library was enough of a time-filler. But eventually, in the summer of 1964 Jackie emerged into full participation. The comparison to the Girl Guides is irresistible, for the classes of 'Beautiful People', as with the Guides, are established with just as ridiculous rigorous examinations. The New Yorkers wanted her for their own. She had already become well known to them in her single years, and during her time as a rich Senator's wife she had discovered for herself the joys of rich and beautiful women, the clothes, the calls, the whole caravanserai. The New York smart Manhattan life was her obvious niche.

She had not been interested in a political post and the life of an Eleanor Roosevelt, the other most famous President's widow, interested her not at all. She had made her sacrifice, given up enough for her country and she now settled down to seriously having fun. Despite the gaiety of her new life, Jackie stayed close to the children, ensuring that governess and nannies kept a strict, rather English, rein on them. American children run wild, rarely receiving the slightest discipline from parents, but these were not the sort of children Jackie wanted to have. Her nephew and niece, Anthony and Anna Radziwill who lived and were brought up in London, and attended the Lycée—a strict Anglo-French school attended by many Embassy children in smart Kensington—seemed infinitely more civilised. Most of the help Jackie employed for her children was European, mainly English.

Caroline began attending the Convent of the Sacred Heart, a little way from the flat and also on Fifth Avenue. It was a private Catholic day school, where she was very happy. By seven years old she had already attended three schools. John, not yet at school, was taken out by nannies and nurses, to the children's zoo in Central Park, and to the Bronx Zoo. Soon they were both going to ride in Central Park, just as their mother had.

Jackie herself began to lead the life of the smart New Yorker. She attended lunches and went to some art gallery openings such as the Hay Whitney in the evenings. She began to see old friends, and new ones, instead of just the old Kennedy clan. Salinger, Schlesinger, Sorensen and others were always loyal to her and the Kennedy name, and helped in the furtherance of the Kennedy Library. Such men as Mike Nichols, the talented film director who directed such films as *Who's Afraid of Virginia Woolf* and *The Graduate*, would take her to quiet dinners. Truman Capote, a friend of her sister, would be in the Jackie crowd sometimes, although when he gave a superb ball one November, Jackie did not attend, that month being too sad for her. She saw many other men around, but there was no romance, just the urge to run whenever a Kennedy called. The sympathy for Jack's widow was incredibly and understandably large. Such men as John Kenneth Galbraith, the famous Harvard economist and former Ambassador to India, Roswell Gilpatric, former Under Secretary of Defence, and George Plimpton, among others, were all friends—all of them, beside Mike Nichols, men at least fifteen years older than herself. Jackie was looking for companionship, but more than that she was looking for security and it was said that with every man she has selected she has been looking for a father figure.

Eventually, after a fantastic few weeks in Seville for the *feria*, when Jackie had stayed with the Duchess of Alba, reputed to be one of the richest women in the world, the story broke. Jackie, it was said, was to marry a man at least twenty years older than herself, Antonio y Garrigues, the Spanish Ambassador to the Holy See. The world could not believe it, he seemed too old. The tension and excitement mounted all over the world where those interested in the fate of the widow-queen had eyes and ears. No-one denied the story, or knew whether Jackie had almost said yes or was still making up her mind. Finally, although she was already a woman in her late thirties, her mother, Mrs Janet Auchincloss, categorically denied the rumour. Senor Garrigues, it was noted, never denied the rumours. Perhaps he, too, was in doubt what to say.

Jackie, the gay widow, danced on and on. It was rumoured that her voice dropped even lower at dinner, so men would have to cluster round to listen to her. Women were jealous of her, even, it was said, the Kennedy women. The Kennedy women and the Bouvier women could not have been more different, particularly in looks. Eunice, Pat and Jean strongly resemble their brothers. They have that aquiline face with sharp eyes, and look slightly tough, capable women. Jackie and Lee by comparison look a lot more feminine, more delicate, more in need of protection. Both had married prominent husbands, Jackie in her marriage to a young Senator, and Lee first in her marriage to a successful Manhattan business-man, and second to Prince Stanislas Radziwill an aristocrat from Poland, who has lived in exile in England since the war. Whereas, the Kennedy girls have married men who worked for their brother Jack at one time. Eunice married Sargent

E

Shriver, already in the Joseph Kennedy dynasty when he married her, and managed some of her father's business; Jean, in marrying Stephen Smith, married an astute businessman and long-armed organiser for her brother's campaign; and Pat married, and has now divorced, the actor Peter Lawford, a handsome charmer who spread the word of Kennedy around Hollywood, particularly amongst Frank Sinatra's clan.

All the girls, though Jean and Pat were her strongest friends amongst them, were slightly apart from her now. Like the rest of the world, everyone could believe her in the role of widow, but when, quite naturally, she wanted to come out of widowhood, and entered the smart, gay world of New York—they remembered their brother, dead, and the manner of his death.

Bobby, the eldest, and the closest to her after Jack's assassination also worried about her, but felt that after her great strength, her majesty and bravery, she was entitled to a 'free ride for life'. But America and the Kennedys were reluctant to let her go.

As yet nothing in her life had become serious. Jackie was the flirt her father had been, but always restrained. She went out with many men, reputedly breaking many hearts, but America watched her as if a naughty daughter. They would cluck and sigh, but loved her all the same, as did the Kennedys. But in 1967 she hurried to England with Bobby for yet another funeral. Lady Harlech had died in a car crash whilst driving on their estate in Wales. David, Lord Harlech, had rushed to Jackie's side when her husband had died, and Jackie was swift to go to him. A new life was rising from this latest tragedy. The merry widow's waltz played on.

Chapter 8

WE LOVE BOBBY

ANOTHER Kennedy was on the road. This one was saved from the sort of criticisms Jack had faced, directed at his youth, religion and wealth. His elder brother had disproved the comments. He attracted the same sort of crowds which took him to their hearts at once. There were other resemblances which were startling. Bobby would speak and some of the Bostonian accents would make you catch your breath. He would look at you straight, and those eyes, so sure in their search for truth, for the right thing, would make you scared to look straight back into them. From some angles they would almost look alike. If Robert minded being compared to his brother he never showed it. The love and loss were still there. His strength had shown itself during the time between the terrible afternoon in Dallas and the pomp of the funeral in Washington. Where his brother's widow wanted him, he would miraculously appear. When she talked, he listened. His face reflected his stoicism.

Jackie, after the assassination, became even more superstitious. Robert returned to the theme he had felt stirring within the family during the forties, at the time of the deaths of Joe Jr. and Kathleen, and the removal of Rosemary from their lives. The thought recurred to him that the Kennedys in their success and luck, looks and thrusting ambition were unfavourably marked out. As he himself said, 'Someone up there doesn't like us much.'

For a short while there was a lull. But with the tragedies of the children Jackie and Jack wanted so much, and then the horrifying stroke their father suffered, rendering him paralysed and almost speechless, they all felt Fate was once more against them. But none of them had allowed the feeling of doom to affect their aims. Jack got his Presidency, Robert became Attorney General, and Ted took over the 'Kennedy Seat' in the Senate. This was the senatorship of Massachusetts, which his brother had held before him. Despite their success, or perhaps, they thought, because of it, they had more bad luck; Patrick Bouvier Kennedy who had lived, only to die a few hours later, seemed to them an ultimate proof of doom. They were not to know that only three months later the biggest blow would fall. November is still a month during which the clan form together and visit the Arlington graveside. In his new position as head of the family, Robert felt overcome by inertia. He was disconsolate and sad as he thought of his brother and the past, and to him the toneless leadership of the present. Though he always felt he was as doomed as the rest of his family, he continued in his work. Ted was to break his back in an air crash that sent the family to their rosaries, though he survived after hospital care. Robert survived by throwing himself back into the political scene again. But he started to feel further and further doomed when those close to him, other than Kennedys died around him. His parents-in-law, the Skakels, were killed in an air crash. Their own death was followed by that of their son, his brother-in-law. As a final terrifying episode, his widow was lunching at her home when some food lodged in her windpipe. She choked to death. Robert by now tossed it off in jokes and with ancient verse. He often quoted the lines from Aeschylus, 'Men are not made for safe havens.' The last death had finally convinced him that Fate was divine. He walked out into his. He also shouldered the enormous burden of the safe-keeping of Jackie and her children. Jackie could never find solace with Ted the way she could with Robert and his father. She needed the experience, the knowledge and security of older men. Robert let her use his home as a happy dumping ground for herself and the children. And she spent much time at what was to be her first home at Hickory Hill whilst she lived in her last home in Washington.

The lives of Jackie and Ethel could not be more different. But of all the sisters in the clan they were the most compatible. They were so different in character and tastes that there was no rivalry. Ethel had no desire to experience the social scene. Nevertheless, she used every ounce of natural talent to dress flatteringly, and to keep herself Kennedy trim and brown, like her husband, with plenty of exercise and sunshine.

Under Jackie's and Rose's guidance she was led to Jackie's favourite couturiers, but the cute little girl look never disappeared. Amazingly, she looked as young as ever. Some of the sophistication rubbed off, but at heart she was maternal; she had ten children, Jackie only two. The Hickory Hill house was decorated in American style. The rooms were full of comfortable sofas and television sets. Jackie's homes were elegant French versions with little American styling, where tea-time was tea *à l'anglais* with *petit beurre* biscuits. Jackie's houses were in smart city streets, with pretty paved courtyards; Ethel's was a stout family home of the sort that is full of dogs, babies and old friends. Jackie, fascinated by artists and interested in the arts, used her ability to introduce the best of them into the White House and around her. Ethel did not understand, or feel at ease with, intellectuals. She preferred to organise barbecues and outdoor parties.

Jackie learnt from her capacity to cope with the children, educating them to the best of her ability within the home. Jackie said of this, 'Making the learning process part game, part work, brings excitement to the child and eagerness to do well . . . The praise that comes from a parent encourages the child more.' She herself had benefited from this sort of instruction. She watched Ethel cope with dinner for seven children, encouraging each of them to recount their day to her, and saw her sister-in-law's elder children growing up well-behaved and intelligent. She used Ethel's techniques when Caroline and

John were born. She also noticed and marvelled at Ethel's piety. The first moment they met after Jack was killed, Ethel assured her with true faith that Jack was in Heaven, happy. Jackie, still in turmoil, envied her belief. The funeral Jackie conducted was one of dignity, pomp and sorrow. Ethel had suggested black borders be left off the prayer cards, she thought funerals too should be joyful. Her house was filled with religious objects, Lalique crucifixes, beautiful rosaries and mantillas for the children. The children, too, were brought up strictly in the faith, and attended all weddings, funerals and christenings, often being godmothers and godfathers to one another. Jackie was less strong in her faith. She was more inclined to worship in solitude. She would spend time alone in the countryside, just gazing down at her husband's grave. She was more afraid of death, and felt, like her husband at the funeral of little Patrick, that it was a great loneliness. That was why she wished to place her most beloved keepsake, her wedding ring, with her husband, almost for company, and why they both put a medallion into Patrick's coffin. To them there was no reason to surrender life joyfully. Those children she had given birth to in vain, the still-born baby girl in 1956 and Patrick, were later moved to be with their father, one on either side of his grave.

The relationship between the four of them had always been close. The sisters-in-law were thrown together not only on clan occasions but by the overriding urge for the brothers to meet, to talk, to plan. When the Kennedy foursome was turned into a triangle, they all aided one another. Jackie and the children came to Hickory Hill for the weekends, leaving the watchers of the Georgetown streets. Bobby was at his most relaxed with them, playing with them and teaching them to swim. Jackie felt the same trust in him as her children did. He was always the one closest to Jack. She loved him most. The large house was full of understanding and sympathy for her.

Growing out of the stunned stage of widowhood, she

eventually grew out of the quiet stage too. She knew she would be all right even without Robert's continual presence, and besides, his political office was New York, he was their representative in the Senate. The Robert Kennedys also had a flat in smart Manhattan, only a few blocks from hers on Fifth Avenue. Sadly the Kennedys and the Washingtonians saw her leave. Washington, like a maiden aunt, was beloved, but bored her. She wanted the big city, and her life there offered much for the consternation of Robert Kennedy. He was often in the town and they kept in close touch, but he could not fail to note the gossip columns discussing her dates with such-and-such and so-and-so, and sometimes, embarrassingly, they would bump into each other.

There was one acquaintance who caused them no embarrassment. Jackie had struck up a close friendship with an old and dear friend, David Ormsby Gore, the Lord Harlech and ex-Ambassador of the United Kingdom to the Court of King John at Washington. He had known something of the horror and tragedy that Jackie herself had known. His wife, to whom he had been married for more than twenty years, had died in a car crash on their Welsh estate. They had both been great friends of the Kennedys, all the Kennedys, recreating a special relationship between the two countries that had been missing for years. They were both well-born. They were intelligent men who were widely read, but not pedants, who had power but were not corruptible, who were attractive but were not dandies.

The European style of the Kennedy household attracted the Harlechs as a home-from-home. Though older than the Kennedys, they had much in common. Amidst the politicians, this was a couple Jackie liked very much. When Lady Harlech was killed, Jackie accompanied Bobby to Britain for the funeral. Eventually, after she had attended the funeral and had returned to her home country, Lord Harlech followed. His memories were too much at home. His children, all almost grown up, led their own lives which were highly publicised in the English press. He enjoyed the company of his avant garde, nonconformist children, but it was not enough. He went to America where they had seen happier times. They came together at first because it was so obvious. Both aesthetes, Jackie Kennedy and Lord Harlech decided to travel round Italy.

They enjoyed each others' company well enough, but it was hardly a sparkling romance. It was rather a convergence of two lost people. Jackie reputedly confided in a friend, 'It was like going out with a walking encyclopaedia.' She wanted the snap, crackle, and pop of the discotheque world of high society. The English Lord was simply too brainy!

Throughout her friendship, for this was all it ever was, with Lord Harlech, she had continued to see her other men-friends, such as Mike Nicholls, an old friend of her sister Lee.

Lee had been slow to emerge. Now the last word in sophistication, she enjoyed the smart sets and their meanderings round Europe. She rather disliked America for long stays, preferring civilized old countries such as England, where she had her London house in Westminster. It was a small terrace house in Buckingham Gate, with a minute garden behind. Her close friends numbered the magnates of Europe. Gianni Aggelli, for example, head of Fiat, the giant Italian car company, or Aristotle Onassis.

It was said that her brother-in-law, the President, had been particularly worried by rumours about Onassis and the mischievous young Lee. When dispatching his wife to her cruise in the *Ionian* in the summer of 1963, he had recommended it both as a holiday, and as a way of dissuading Lee from pursuing her relationship with Onassis. Onassis, successful and immensely rich, had been in trouble with the New York authorities. As far as shipping mortgages alone were concerned there was no danger, but he had a reputation as a buccaneer rather than as a businessman. He would be too close for comfort to the President of the United States, if the rumours were to be believed. Lee had already been divorced, receiving Jackie's help over an annulment; only after this could she go through with a church wedding to her new husband, Prince Stanislas Radziwill. Whether the rumours were true or not we shall never know. Nonetheless, the trip worked and comment died down. In other ways, too, the cruise was a success; Jackie came back invigorated, and ready to face the beginning of the campaign in Texas.

Onassis had been one of the first to hasten to the White House after that day, dining there on the night of the funeral. He had offered Jackie the use of his boat whenever she wished. He had also promised to look her up in New York. This he did, until once again a Bouvier was becoming involved with the moneyed Greek.

Again, a Kennedy got 'hopping mad'. When Jackie told her brother-in-law she was thinking of remarrying, he was horrified. In May of 1968 he was concentrating his efforts on a Presidential primary barnstorming, the like of which had not been seen since his brother's efforts and success in 1960. And though willing to allow his sister-in-law everything after all she had gone through, he could not take this. He entreated her to wait, at least until the Presidential elections had come and gone. He hoped to avoid harm to the Kennedy image—he also hoped that she would forget Onassis.

Jackie was still undecided.

Putting aside personal worries, Bobby began slowly to move the nation with his appeals. The minority groups, the oppressed and the poor, came to love him. His wife was to bear another child, their eleventh. He strove to be as good as his brother and battled on. This time he was against more persuasive opponents than his brother had confronted. The other liberal on the platform was hard to beat. Bobby's own reputation was also formidable: he was tough, ruthless, self-centred. These were the qualities he had shown to the Democrats when he had organised his brother's campaign. They had understood that the candidate would be above this; the second in command would take the brick bats for him and wield the hatchet. The Democratic forces could not forget that quickly, nor could they forget their relationship to politics which their father had preached. First of all Joe would go into politics; if something happened to him it would be Jack's turn, if something happened to him, Robert would be next; and if something happened to him, it would be Teddy. Bobby treasured a cigarette box given him by his brother when he became President. It said, 'When I'm through, how 'bout you?' He was answering that appeal. He lost in Oregon, but he won in California. He stood making a quickly prepared thank-you speech in Los Angeles. His wife, in the early stages of pregnancy, dressed in a trim, white Courréges dress stood by. The cheers came. He reached out and touched the people. He turned to go out by a kitchen. He walked through a tunnel of people. And then looked down the hard edge straight barrel of a gun. They had said it could never happen again, but in the same hotel where Nixon had conceded defeat to his brother Jack in 1960, he conceded the world. Twenty-five hours later he was dead.

The widows travelled across the country with the coffin in a plane. They went to New York, Jackie's most beloved home. The brightly-lit scene received him again. They returned to Fifth Avenue and the funeral, which Ethel tried to convert into a joyful occasion. They heard again that famous cracked, sharp voice, now in Teddy's mouth, reading an ovation to yet another murdered brother.

While standing on the pavement outside the huge Catholic church on that famous street, Jackie, short-sleeved and wearing a black mantilla looked straight into the camera's eye. The words in her eyes were, '*J'accuse*'. A long way off a motor-cycle exhaust snorted loudly. She started, and looked very frightened.

Chapter 9

DADDY O

THEY were painting the little church. The buckets of the grey wash stood outside the building. The men brushed it on jovially, taking care about their task. It shone pale grey, and then, miraculously, as if the Mediterranean sun had some magic washing-powder ingredient, dried to perfect white. Flowers seemed to be everywhere, some flown in, others gathered with bunches of leaves from all over the island. The path started to become neater. Activity, activity. The place resounded with the noise of people rushing about; the locals were busy, and the master was watching everything very carefully.

Aristotle Socrates Onassis, at sixty-two, awaited an avalanche of the world's press into his private life, a new bride and the Greek Orthodox wedding ceremony, not for the first time. For Jacqueline Bouvier Kennedy, aged thirty-nine, was coming out of the night of tragedy, and the glad sad evenings of the merry widow, into the day, into the sun, the harsh bright Greek sun. And as the harsh bright eyes of the ever-curious world looked down on the lush isle of Scorpios, the inevitable question was asked . . . why?

Jackie and Tellis (her name for him from the Greek Aristotle) first met in 1959 on board the beautiful yacht *Christina*, which Onassis had named after his daughter. He had bought the boat in 1954, which had previously been the Canadian frigate *Stormont*. The sixteen hundred ton ship was soon converted into the world's most luxurious yacht at a North German shipyard. The ship has the smart white accommodation ladder of all international luxury yachts, and it is as perfect, and as immaculate as the day the owner brought her to Greece. Each of her nine suites is named after a Greek island. In cyrillic script their names are inscribed on the doors. *Chios*, the favourite suite of Sir Winston Churchill, with a stunningly beautiful marble bathroom, and *Crete*, the adjoining suite occupied by his male nurses. *Ithaca*, where such women as Lady Churchill, Greta Garbo, Maria Callas and Jackie Kennedy herself have slept. Other suites are called *Mykonos*, *Santorin*, *Rhodes*, *Corfu* and *Andros*. Each double suite has been designed and furnished by a different artist. Each has bathrooms of marble, with such luxurious items as wash basins with gold fish-mouth taps, lavatories and bidets all in such perfectly cut marble that each object becomes a work of art. And yet each suite is very different.

Perhaps the most unique of all is Onassis's own. It is of perfect Siena marble, the bathroom a replica of the one in King Minos's palace at Knossos. Strange that King Minos whose ships, four thousand years ago, gave him the mastery of the Greek seas, should lend his bathroom design to the master of the Greek seas of the modern age! It is made of perfect tortoise-shell brown shaded Siena marble. The frescoes and mosaics are exact replicas of the brilliantly coloured flying fish and dolphins from the long lost palace of King Minos at Knossos on the island of Crete. This was discovered at the end of the last century by an English archaeologist, Sir Arthur Evans, and many modern scholars believe it to have been the legendary Atlantis. Despite its ancient connections, connections in this the master suite with the modern world have not been over-looked, three of the *Christina's* forty-two telephone extensions are in the owner's cabin.

A delicate circular stairway, its height nearer three storeys than decks, leads to the cabins. Its sides are lined with glass cases holding some of Onassis's enormous collection of tiny models of almost every famous ship, including Noah's Ark and the *Kon-Tiki*. The colour scheme is gold, and Wedgwood blue. The staircase also leads to the big study. Dominating this room with its many books—some of them by Onassis's friends, like Sir Winston Churchill—heavily framed in gold, is the famous painting by El Greco of the Madonna and Angel, jokingly referred to as 'El Greco's El Greco' by his friends. Underneath this is an elegant wooden desk, decorated with gold handles and mouldings. The walls are panelled. On them hang mementoes, souvenirs, presents from some of the world's famous men, Russian ikons, swords in gold scabbards and whaling trophies. This is where Onassis can work whilst at play, this is one of the places where he can keep in touch with half a dozen capitals all over the world.

For all the exquisiteness of his surroundings, Onassis, being a typically gregarious Greek, is still a man's man. There is an excellent bar, the walls of which are a magnet to any man interested in naval matters—parchment maps, some of them very old, and more of the model ships adorn this comfortable retreat. The bar stools are covered in white whaleskin, said to be taken from the most sensitive part of that greatest of mammals. Another fairly masculine retreat, though perhaps more for the studious, is the very English smoking-room on the poop deck. It has a large grand piano and an open fireplace of lapis lazuli, costing nearly two pounds per square inch. There are deep chairs with soft cushions, gentle restful colours, the air usually full of the aroma of expensive Havana cigars, fine champagne cognac, and the talk of some of the most powerful men in the world. When outsiders are around their faces do not crease with anything more than a big grin, at one of Ari's (another of his nicknames) famous jokes. But the telephone messages passed on a silver tray belie, if it were even possible in such magnificent, if over-lush, surroundings, the impression of apparent casualness of some old friends gathered around for a simple holiday. The forty-two extensions on the *Christina* are often employed both by Onassis and his busy guests, for the *Christina* is the centre of his world, his first home, despite other bases in Paris, London and New York, not his escape from it. Whereas some rich and powerful men use their yachts as retreats from the world, Onassis uses his as a magnificent floating office, the centre of his dynamic empire.

When Jacqueline Kennedy first set foot on the *Christina* she, like most of the other distinguished guests, often quite large yacht owners themselves, took the conducted tour round the yacht with the proud host. It was probably the dining-room that caught her immediate attention, for it is furnished in the style of Louis XV. She saw the priceless eighteenth century furniture, the high cane-backed carved chairs, their arms carved with gold intaglio (like the ones she herself purchased for her first home as Mrs J F Kennedy). The round table, and draped bottle-green curtains reaching down to the marble blocked floor, the four panels round the wall depicting the seasons, painted by Vertes, made this her favourite room. She had confided once to a close friend, 'The period in history I would have liked to have lived in most was France at the time of Louis XV.' This was the dazzling, elegant epoch of the Enlightenment when Voltaire and Montesquieu conversed in the salons of the gilded aristocracy; when the first encyclopaedia was produced, and moral life ebbed to a new low of decadence.

She also loved the children's room, almost unchanged since Alexander, Onassis's now twenty-one year old son, and Christina herself, now eighteen, played in it. The walls are painted to tell a story of a French schoolgirl, a small electric organ is still in its place and, by its side, a music box disguised as a Monte Carlo fruit machine. The room is a simple playroom although it was designed for two of the most fortunate young people in the world, a place where the children of the rich can run, scream, play and shout without hindrance, safely out of the way of the ship's famous swimming pool cum dance floor. The floor is electrically raised or dropped to the right level. The pool is decorated with a famous scene from the

King Minos palace of the Bull and the Dancing Acrobats or bull-dancers. It is an enlarged reproduction of the famous fresco of the mythological story of the Minotaur, half-bull, half-man, son of King Minos, who devoured the young Athenian youths and girls offered in his tribute, until he was killed by the legendary first king of Athens, young Theseus.

But Jackie's first look at the yacht was a quick one. In fact she and her husband, the then Senator for Massachussets, had been invited for a cocktail party, and she could hardly stay below decks for long. Tina and Aristotle Onassis were entertaining a very distinguished guest on board. At this time the large yacht was moored in Monte Carlo harbour, and Sir Winston Churchill with his wife, his daughter Diana Sandys and private secretary, Montague Brown, were ensconced on it. They had returned from the Canary Islands, the first of the many Onassis-Churchill cruises.

Onassis knew Jack Kennedy, as he had met him several times in Washington and New York. When he heard that he was in the vicinity visiting his father, Joseph, he immediately invited him to the cocktail party that he and Tina, daughter of another Greek shipping millionaire, Stavros Livanos, were giving on the deck of the *Christina* that evening. He spoke to the young Kennedy in a very uncharacteristic way, 'I shall have to ask you to leave not later than seven-thirty' he said— Winston Churchill had a strict regimen, with dinner each evening always sharp at eight-fifteen, and Onassis had no wish to disturb his distinguished guest's timetable. Onassis, solicitous for his guests, took care to be there himself when Sir Winston needed a blanket to fend off a sharp sea wind, or his stick for a walk round the deck. Thus it was that he told JFK, 'I am afraid your visit will have to be a very short one.'

When Jack and Jackie arrived, Onassis announced him to Sir Winston, saying, '*Young* Kennedy is here, would you like to meet him?' Churchill's face lit up. He had, of course, met Jack's father during his ambassadorship in London and had heard of Jack's high hopes for the future. Onassis settled them both in a corner. Immediately they were deep in political discussion, Churchill asking Kennedy a dozen questions. 'What are your chances in the election?' he asked. Jack Kennedy replied that because of his Catholicism, the fight would not be an easy one. Churchill replied, 'If that's the only difficulty you can always change your religion and still remain a good Christian.' Kennedy laughed and the conversation continued on other political topics. They got on so well that it was long after dinner time, near nine o'clock, when the Kennedys finally left. Thereafter Onassis and Kennedy saw one another occasionally, when Onassis was in New York or Washington. Onassis, however, since his romance with Maria Callas, had required something of a nimbus of scandal and gossip. He had fought some earlier skirmishes with the US Maritime Administration, and there was his feud with Prince Rainier of Monaco; he was not at all the man for a close White House friendship. Nonetheless, the family kept in touch. Lee Bouvier Radziwill, based in London, saw Onassis far more frequently at social gatherings, and Onassis always felt close to the Kennedys. In April 1961, Sir Winston Churchill sailed on the *Christina* up the Hudson River to New York. America gave him an overwhelming welcome, distinguished visitors came aboard to present their good wishes and towards the end of the day, when the telephone rang on board, Churchill was happy to learn that the person on the other end was the President. During their conversation Jack Kennedy offered his Presidential plane, Air Force One, to carry Churchill from New York to Washington and then back. But Sir Winston had to decline, he felt he was a little too old for an unscheduled air trip, and besides, the visit would have had to be short, as he was due to return home. He begged to be excused, and the President was sympathetic. He had a brief word with Onassis, and wished them both God Speed. The next time Jack Kennedy was to telephone the *Christina* was to speak to his wife, Jackie.

In the late summer of 1963, Lee Radziwill was a guest of Onassis at an Athens dinner party when the sad news came through that Jackie's new-born baby, Patrick, had died. Onassis immediately suggested that Jackie might like to recuperate on a cruise on his yacht. He placed it at her entire disposal and Jackie, encouraged by Lee, gratefully accepted. This was the third child that had died, and her husband had longed for a second son. Physically, too, the ordeal had been gruelling. There were also rumours that her sister was far too involved with the Greek and that her husband the President was worried about it.

When she got to Greece, she refused to travel unless her host would accompany herself and her guests. The party included the Radziwills, and Franklin D Roosevelt Jr. and his wife. Onassis agreed, but determined to stay in the background, insisting, 'Mrs Kennedy is the Captain.' In fact, he kept so much out of the way that Franklin Roosevelt had to tell him that Jackie had noticed his reticence, and thought it most touching, but quite unnecessary. After that he went with them whenever they made a shore landing. On this cruise under the Mediterranean sun, sailing through the island archipelagos of the Aegean and Ionian seas, they visited Istanbul and Ithaca, and Onassis was an assiduous guide.

In America there was an outcry at the cruise. Jackie's husband wished her to return, but they must have come to an agreement, for the cruise continued with Jackie as the star of the party. The President was amused when Lee wrote to him in mock complaint that Jackie had been laden with presents; whereas from Zolotas, Ari's favourite jeweller, she herself had only received 'three dinky little bracelets that Caroline wouldn't wear to her own birthday party'.

During the cruise, Jackie would often speak to her husband in Washington by telephone, and she wrote to him that she realised that she was enjoying a privilege which he could never have—the absence of tension. She wished she could bestow it on him. This was what Onassis gave to her, after all her trials and tribulations and the terrible memories America had for her, with another coffin to remind her of her sorrow. After the sun and the quiet, she could go back, stronger and healthier. She had, she confided to her friends, so many happy memories.

Then, only a month later, the memories of sunburnished Ionian landscapes were blotted from her mind in the tragedy that was to isolate 22 November 1963 from everything that had gone before. After Jack's funeral, Onassis was one of the first people to visit her. He had been in Hamburg on the day of the assassination, attending the launching of one of his new tankers, the fifty-thousand ton *Olympic Chivalry*, and was just about to sit down to the celebration dinner at the Hotel Vier Jahreszeiten when the news broke of the murder of his friend, President Kennedy. The meal turned into a wake. Onassis, an admirer and friend of the family once more so tragically struck down, was anxious to be away.

After Jackie's period of widowhood, when she devoted her time to her children alone, men came into her life again. Who was to guess that her last beau and her second husband was to be a sixty-two-year-old, foreign shipping magnate. The world had, it felt, a right to question why. Jackie had become, in the public eye, the Dowager Queen of the United States. They were determined she was not to make a morganatic marriage. She must marry someone equal both to her high status and to her dead husband. Thus the friendship between Jackie and Lord Harlech had been looked upon by Americans in a kindly light. He was regarded by them as suitable and they felt he was welcome to come and visit any time. Like over-solicitous parents, their reaction could not have been more horrified when they heard of Jackie's plans.

Firstly, Onassis was foreign! The fact that America is still a melting pot of immigrant nationalities, while most Americans can trace their citizenship only two generations, was irrelevant. Lord Harlech, of course, was a foreigner, too, but he was a

Lord, and was so obviously a gentleman. Onassis, although a gentleman, is not such a conventional one. Lord Harlech was a figure of tragedy. His wife, to whom he had been devoted, had died three years after John F Kennedy, in a motoring accident on the family estate in Wales. Onassis was a figure of scandal. His open liaison with Maria Meneghini Callas the prima donna of the world's opera stages, the cause of his divorce, and herself still married had given the *papparazi* a news story for the last nine years. In fact, the story had only ended with a final culminating row in the late summer of 1968.

The reason for the break was Jackie. Onassis had been seeing her a lot in Hyannis Port and Newport, Rhode Island, in Manhattan and her mother's home, the Auchincloss estate, and Callas probably heard the rumour 'Ari would forget Maria Callas in a minute if he thought he had a chance with Jackie!' And after almost nine years of the romance, she still married, and he seemingly the determined bachelor, she had had enough.

Lord Harlech had been a close friend of Jack Kennedy. As the esteemed British Ambassador to the US, he and the President had kept open the special relationship between the two countries. Ari Onassis, who had had trouble with the US Maritime Administration on ships' mortgages, was definitely too controversial a man to be friendly with a President. Nor did Onassis fit into the mould of the 'Beautiful People'. He himself admitted, 'Jackie likes tall, thin men, I hardly think I fit the description!' He was already, at sixty-two, very grey, a few inches shorter than Jackie, slightly stocky with a muscular Greek build and deeply lined face, no doubt a well-dressed man, but definitely not an elegant one. The public felt their princess had been left with the frog instead of the Prince. They were not happy, such headlines as 'Jackie, how could you?' went eddying round the world. Even the American astronauts who happened to be orbiting the earth at that time could only say 'Oh my!'

Lee Radziwill herself explains the American public's reaction, 'Had my sister married a young, blonde, rich Anglo-Saxon, Americans would have been quite content.' American disapproval of Onassis was also based on his exhibitionism. He spent his money freely. He enjoyed all the luxuries money could buy. He invested his money, not in libraries and academies, but in new financial ventures to make yet more money. His ruthless pursuit of pleasure, and the attendant privacy that must go with it for a man of his position, involved the re-building of a fantastic yacht, the buying of his own Greek island, a constant suite at Claridges, a home in the Avenue Foch in Paris, a suite at the Pierre Hotel, New York, whence he could, as much as possible, slip in and out of countries whenever business or pleasure called. Americans of wealth, on the contrary, devote their money to founding charitable institutions, backing political parties and generally revealing a rather Puritan attitude to their money, guilt. The Americans' word for Onassis is a buccaneer, or by some, even pirate; the word conjures up adventure, but slightly sharp, shady adventure.

The most overwhelming feeling the Americans had on that Thursday, October 19, was that Jackie was leaving them. Lithe and slim, her hair high and wide round her shining face, wearing a chic grey outfit, and flanked by her beautiful children she walked out onto Fifth Avenue for the last time as Mrs Jacqueline Kennedy before driving to the airport named after her late husband. America felt deserted. As she mounted the steps of the Olympia Airways jet they watched her ride out of their sky, as she had ridden into it, the most dramatic heroine in American history five long years ago. Dramatically, and almost as tragically, they felt bereft.

America had forgotten to look at the real Jackie. They had looked only at the myth. For a woman who loves balls, parties and fun, Jackie could not have nestled in the tragic mould America had devised for her for the rest of her life. She, as a debutante, had led the usual empty-headed, gay life of a wealthy, beautiful East Coast girl. Then she grew up and married. Her marriage pushed her, in many ways, into a life she had not really envisaged, even though her husband was a Senator when she married him. Jacqueline Bouvier Kennedy has always liked the limelight, but it was the back street work, the dinners with politicians, the political chat amongst her in-laws, the smiles and waves to throngs of people, hand-shakes, speeches, women's clubs in America—these were in no way Jackie's cup of tea. She had, when she was young, inter-ested herself in the arts, antiques, the theatre and books and music. During her often lonely married life, when her husband was out politicking, or dealing with a crisis, or up at the Senate, or late in his White House office, she would read books voraciously and listen to music late in the night. Her comfort-able room at the White House would often be the last light to go out. So, with her husband's death, the political interest went out of her life.

Her move away from the capital to gayer New York was the first move in her alienation from political life. But then there were also the Kennedys. The clan had their own strict routines, laws and life. The family compound at Hyannis Port was a typical, ambitious, rich, all-American group of families. They played sports, prepared their children for competition, toughened them up for a future which, no doubt, their grandfather, Joseph P Kennedy, was already planning, just as he had encouraged his sons. It was a world of coke, and peanut butter sandwiches, of touch-football, the Catholic church and great extrovert fun and politics. For Jackie, her shyness and unwillingness to participate in this sort of life, and to give this sort of life to her children increased after Jack's death. Instead, although she still returned to Hyannis Port, she found her beaches in Hawaii and other hot spots all over the world. Eventually, always making the moves on her own began to pall, and even when her escorts came, it would produce only a rash of photographs, and comment. It also became very expensive.

Jackie is, of course, by no means poor, but although there are the Kennedy millions, there are also millions of Kennedys. Much of the money left to her by her late husband is tied up with trustees; to these Jackie must give full financial accounts, for much of the money is for Caroline and John. By no means is she scraping the financial barrel, but for someone like Jackie, who craves excitement, new faces, new places, the latest action, the newest clothes, money does not go far. Besides, however far the money takes you, there was, for Jackie, always someone with a camera, someone who would watch her so much that she could never relax. Her control is remarkable; for someone who virtually chain smokes (Salem is her favourite brand), she manages never to have a cigarette in her hand in a photograph. By now Jackie had had enough.

For these reasons it was not so incredible that she married Aristotle Socrates Onassis. He is a well known apolitical man. So much so that there has been an outcry about his four hundred million pound deal with the present Greek dictatorship. The critics should know by now that he deals with any government. He, too, likes a full social round, and when he is not working he dedicates himself to it with all the gusto that goes into making him the multi-millionaire he is. Despite his age, top night-spots and fashionable haunts still entrance him. When in New York, his favourites number Trader Vic's or PJ's as well as the snob Plaza Hotel. He can take Jackie away from America. She can break away from the public role that she submitted to better as a young woman when her husband, the President, was alive. And also there is money. An Everest of dollars, with which she can do whatever she wishes. Nothing is too much for her now . . . both her own choice of spending and the fantastic gifts Onassis will shower upon her. A one hundred and sixty room 'cottage' on Scorpios is his next buy for her. And then there is privacy. For the first time Jackie can live outside the range of the flashbulb. No-one, except the Onassis servants, lives on Scorpios. The locals go back by boat to Lefkas each evening and return in the morning. When Onassis bought Scorpios he also bought the two islands through which boats must pass to get to the island, thus no boats or prying cameras can watch Jackie water ski-ing or swimming with her children.

Of course no-one, no-one at all since the wedding, either friend or foe to Jackie, has mentioned the word love. Perhaps when a couple are sixty-two and thirty-nine people just do not refer to them as starry-eyed lovers, and certainly no-one at the wedding described them as such. But it must be remembered that Jackie, as much if not more than most women, needed men—for kindness and care and companionship. She has few women friends. Her sister Lee is her confidante, and she lives in London. And life into middle age without a husband was probably a depressing thought, particularly as yet another of the men with whom she had a close relationship had also been taken away from her. Jackie had been toying with the idea of marrying Onassis before 5 June. He had proposed in May. She told her brother-in-law Bobby of her idea. He, apparently, was 'hopping mad', unusually so for Bobby, who felt that the world had treated her so badly 'she should get a free ride for life'. Of course, Bobby, then still very much in the running for the Presidency, realised, as his brother before him, that Onassis was a liability. His life, and troubles with the US authorities, plus the usual feelings about a suitable husband for Jackie, combined to set him against the idea. Jackie's mind was not made up, however, and the subject was carried no further. Ari would wait for her answer. Once again Fate, in the bullet, in the gun in the hand of a madman, changed her life. She attended Bobby's funeral with a darkness in her heart. The Kennedys were doomed. She must escape, but she must also feel safe. Taken away from her at the age of eight, a father she adored, admired, revered, and for the rest of her life tried to impress, live up to, represented the kind of security in life for which she craved. She had always got on best with older men. Jack Kennedy himself was a little over twelve years older. Her great hits whilst First Lady had been with Nikita Kruschev and Charles de Gaulle, both men well into their sixties. Lord Harlech was several years older. She always said that the person she most admired of the Kennedys was her father-in-law, Joseph P Kennedy. And her greatest praise of any friend was 'that he never let you down'. The public wished her at the side of a beautiful young man. She wanted the safety of older, tender care. Jackie's mind was made up. Over long-distance telephone, in July, she acquiesced to a marriage that she knew the world would hate. But she had looked after the world long enough. Jackie Bouvier Kennedy, not for the first time, readied herself for the altar, and prepared to ignore the headlines. She told her few friends, her sister being one of the first. She finally informed the Kennedys, feeling it was correct to discuss the situation with Ted who had accompanied her on the cruise in the *Christina* only a few months before, in the hope of dissuading his elder sister-in-law from the marriage. She confided in Cardinal Cushing. Then she waited to produce a *fait accompli*. Unfortunately the Press pieced things together. Cushing's words, 'My lips are sealed', to the reporters' open questions, told the story.

Jackie Bouvier was about to change out of the Kennedy costume, which by now had become a shroud, into a wedding dress.

Thus the hurrying and scurrying of the island, on which Onassis had, as yet, done almost nothing in the way of building, content to own it and sail around it in proprietary pride. The little church was set amid cypress trees. The warm sun of Greece burnt down on the earth. The scent of herbs, common on all Greek hillsides, mixed with the headier ones of international perfumes. Onassis's sister, Artemis, arrived to look over the scene of the wedding, and with her the rest of the

Onassis coterie of relatives. Jackie was again to marry into a large family.

The large plane, usually filled with tourists come to catch the last of the Dionysiac sun, descended from the sky onto the tarmac at Androvida. She was first down the steps with a quick embrace for her future husband. She had to bend to give it to him. He warmly welcomed her, the two children who seemed a little puzzled, and her sisters-in-law and, with great ceremony, her mother.

The name Onassis is well known. But many of those who caused such a hue and cry about the wedding know little about Greeks or Greece. The romantic Ari had made a practice of sending flowers or love-tokens every day he had been away from Jackie since May. Again, like a younger man, he can still do the *hassapiko* and the *zimbekiko*, energetic dances to the background of the bouzouki, which are especially popular among the Greeks of Turkey (his background).

Greeks are, by nature, intensely political animals, but Onassis, it seems, is an exception. Living apart from his nation's political vicissitudes, his vast fleets are even now registered under the flags of convenience of Panama and Liberia so as to avoid paying tax to Greece. The Greeks are fond of money. That Onassis is no exception is indisputable. Onassis should not be underrated. His knowledge of Greek literature and history is typical of a man belonging to an intensely patriotic people. He is vital, enthusiastic and constantly interested in new things. Unlike Jack Kennedy, he will go to the town's top hotspots, follow the smart crowd, and pamper his women. He is a loyal member of the jet set. For his wife he would do everything. Recently they went to P J Clark's, an old-fashioned but fashionable restaurant-bar in Manhattan. When Jackie got up from her table to go to the ladies room, fifty per cent of the room (the female half), rose as well. The curiosity has not abated. The ladies room was jammed, and Jackie was embarrassed. Ari, wishing to protect her from everything, offered the owner a million dollars for the place. The owner refused—but what a compliment for Jackie!

It is said by many they are already splitting apart. They rumour the children cannot accept him, because their hero father is too alive in their memories. They say that the two made a pact, when they married, to spend only the convenient times together, summer on the yacht sailing in the Aegean, Christmas and perhaps Easter. But the rest of the time they would be apart; Jackie in New York, seeing to her children's education, keeping them close to the other Kennedys, Onassis, busy as always with his business. But people who really know the couple say this is complete fabrication. Aristotle Onassis is a proud man, he will not be a mere cipher, a signer of cheques. And Jackie really needs him, glad to share her life with an older man who can offer her the security she has always needed.

Jackie, arriving in Greece with her small Kennedy retinue, thence travelled on to Skorpios and the boat. There she stayed on the yacht with as many of the others as the boat's lush accommodation could hold. Then the family group came ashore. The press, desperate for the biggest story in months, crowded round. All the bride-to-be would say was that, 'Tellis and I are very happy these days'. These days were certainly better than some of the black yesterdays. But the crowd, forgetting these and thinking of the young, purposeful man, cried. The West German *Bild Zeitung* shouted 'America Has Lost a Saint!' from its headlines. France's *Le Monde* called Onassis 'the antithesis' of John Kennedy's hopes for a 'less cruel world'.

All the know-alls came out of hiding. 'He's not a gentleman' said one acquaintance. And when Dean Papadeas, of the American Greek Orthodox Church, was asked what he could say about Onassis after the news of the impending marriage broke, he replied, 'Not very much, I married him the first time'.

Nonetheless, Jackie Kennedy loved him enough, knowingly

to defy the Catholic Church. She will be forever in an irregular position, and she will be unable to participate fully in her children's religious life. And Jackie loved him enough to go through the strange service. The Greek Orthodox wedding ceremony is very beautiful, but strange to those who do not know it. Understanding this, Tellis asked for the service to be partly in English, partly in Greek.

On Sunday, 20 October, the rain poured down from grey skies over Skorpios. To the Greeks, it was a lucky omen. Rain on a wedding day means good luck and fertility. The bride put on a creamy white suit, the top banded with strips of matching lace, the skirt quite short and pleated, her hair full and high as ever, tied back with a matching ribbon. She took her children, her mother and her sisters-in-law and walked along the deck of the luxurious ship to a motor launch. The widow of John Fitzgerald Kennedy covered her head with a scarf and quickly climbed into a car for the short ride that was to take her to the path leading up to the little chapel of the Holy Virgin. The rain still fell in a fine film, and she clasped her daughter's hand and half ran, half walked up the path to the top. As is customary in wedding services of the Greek Orthodox Church, her husband-to-be awaited her at the door of the church. He kissed her on both cheeks. Aristotle Socrates Onassis, in a smart businessman's navy suit, a white shirt and a red tie, with a sprig of lemon blossom in his buttonhole, smiled as his latest bride with her usual dignity and grace held his hand and walked up to the table in front of the altar, which simply held a bible and two rings. The church was full. The forty guests and the attendant clerics stood in hushed silence among the incense, the dark Byzantine ikons and the gold. Caroline Kennedy and John Fitzgerald Kennedy Jr. stood in the aisle holding long, delicate candles. Between, and slightly behind them, stood Mrs Garoufalidu, sister of the groom, the matron-of-honour. Next to them stood their new step-sister, and brother, Alexander and Christina Onassis. The children wide-eyed, strangers to this ceremony, stood and watched. Ari crossed his right hand to his left side and held Jackie's right hand in his. Greek hymns were sung and prayers were said, and then the rings were exchanged three times, hand to hand, by the priest. White wedding crowns, made in leather to look like twigs and buds, and to be kept by the loving couple as a memento, were crossed above the heads. The couple took three sips of red wine and the guests showered them with petals and rice during the dance of Isaiah, a dance to the gaiety and happiness of marriage. Jacqueline Bouvier Onassis, her husband, the priest and the matron-of-honour danced round the altar three times. The bride and groom smiling and closing their eyes against the flowers and the rice, missiles of fertility. Then the bride stepped on the foot of the groom, her way of balancing the phrase in the wedding service: the woman must obey the man.

The ceremony was over. The bride accepted the kisses of her children and step-children and then quickly followed her husband who began walking back up the aisle; clasping her hand tightly was her daughter Caroline. The bride's mother and the bride had tears in their eyes. The bridal pair emerged, Onassis just a little ahead of Jacqueline and her two children. Then came the handful of press, allowed reluctantly by Jackie to attend, to remember that this was 'a private moment'—a moment she compared in its privacy to birth and death. 'Even though people may be well known, they still hold in their hearts the emotion of a simple person,' she had said.

Offshore, the fight to get to the island continued when flotillas of small boats, carrying pressmen and their cameras, clashed with sailors from the *Christina* and Onassis's special guards. He had begged her to permit a plane-load of selected friendly journalists to cover the wedding, in order to avoid the unseemly fracas that surrounded the ceremony, but her hostility to the press had been strengthened when, on the eve of her wedding, her seven-year old son had been approached, and asked what he thought of his mother's wedding. After the family emerged from the church—the bridal couple not looking at each other but shyly smiling at those waiting outside—they stepped into an open car to drive down to the water front. The groom took the wheel, his bride hugged her daughter close to her. Her son sat in the back seat with his ubiquitous friend, the security man. Back on the boat, a banquet had been prepared. First of all there were drinks and the bouzouki orchestra playing intoxicating melodies of Greece, songs of summer, of love and of parting's sweet sorrows. The young Radziwills, Anna and Anthony, and Sydney Lawford, Caroline's favourite cousin, were companions to the young Kennedys. Just before dinner Jackie waved from the side of the boat, then went below to change into one of the many chiffon and silk outfits she had bought for her trousseau. 'I like these,' she said, 'they make me feel so naughty'. Once again, jewels were her wedding present. But this time the necklace, earrings, bracelet and ring were cut so big, so bright, so brilliant that even this audience gasped, and Caroline rushed to her mother, saying, 'Mummy you're so pretty, they're so pretty'. Mrs Onassis gave her daughter the ring to play with and the little girl threw it into the air to make it sparkle. Diamonds, and rubies large as strawberries; red and white, the colours of the buttonhole labels on the campaign trip to Texas.

The Onassis honeymoon began the next day, when the children returned to New York for school. Accompanied by their aunts and grand-mother, they flew to Athens before going on to New York. The only word heard to break their quiet, child-like solemnity was the frantic call from John, 'Don't let the press in!', from behind the door of his hotel room in Athens. The couple were left alone on the gigantic yacht. A few days later the world saw a film of them, one at each end of a tiny rowing boat, buffeted by the breeze, trying valiantly to cope with the wind-tossed sea.

Chapter 10

AFTERWORDS

JACQUELINE Onassis in her time has been the subject of almost as much newsprint as Jacqueline Lee Bouvier and Jacqueline Bouvier Kennedy before her. But the world was wrong to think of them as three different people. They may wonder how the 'private person', a lover of the tasteful, elegant life, could bind herself so closely to the flamboyant, over-publicised zillionaire. Many people attribute his success with her to this last factor. Perhaps it is because they just do not understand this marriage. They question: how could this woman, who had borne the name of the West's greatest champion of freedom, ally herself to a man whose support of the oppressive military junta was so open? Onassis had never worked so closely with any of the more liberal Greek governments. It was even rumoured that Anne-Marie, the exiled Queen of Greece, had begged Jackie not to let herself be associated with the Colonels. But it should be remembered that Jackie was not interested in politics.

How could a woman of her beauty marry a man old enough to be her father? America has no tradition of women marrying older men, unless they be showgirls with millionaires; whereas in Europe, especially in countries under whose rigid family codes sons wait for all their sisters to be married before taking a wife themselves, it is a common practice.

And why would Onassis want her? He who had long courted Maria Callas and yet seemed more than content with bachelorhood, why had he proposed to her the moment the time was ripe, and waited five months for her answer? To him, she was the summit of contemporary womanhood; his rival Stavros Niarchos, another fabulously wealthy Greek ship-owner (they had both married the daughters of yet another rich Greek shipowner) was an infrequent host to Princess Margaret, and had recently married (and divorced) Charlotte Ford. Onassis, always a competitive, ambitious man—and a collector of celebrities—had been a friend of Mrs Kennedy for some years. Why should he not remove the burdens of the world from the widow and make her his bride?

There is an old, old law of nature. Before certain species of birds mate, the males fly to an adjoining field and battle for territory. The bravest and strongest birds end up with the largest area, and wait and sing. Then the females come and the most desirable gravitate towards the males with the largest territory. The name of this game is security. Had Jacqueline Kennedy simply wanted money, however, or the security that money can buy, there were many other men she could have married, without creating the sort of uproar she so hates. But Aristotle Onassis is a warm, witty man of great enthusiasms and charm. He will offer her complete privacy, complete tranquillity; Jackie, still a loner, spends much time away from her husband. She is a strong, determined woman who insists on seeing her children educated in the United States; on enjoying the Manhattan socialite life she knows and loves so well; on going to Washington each November to pray at two graves in Arlington cemetery.

And this is the secret of Jackie Onassis. Brought up in the smart snob world of the East coast, and wife of a millionaire at the age of twenty-four, she was left much to her own devices during youth and not enough later on. Having the instincts of an aristocratic aesthete and yet a taste for the dilettantism of a debutante; being selfish, yet being strong; being weak, yet being gentle, she is an ideal figure of twentieth century, Western womanhood. That she did not become a small photograph on the inside pages of out-of-news papers is simply that, in the last analysis, when the spotlight turned on her she outshone it with a black, shining light of her own. It is to her undying credit that she did so.